What Ministry Leaders Are Saying About *FireBride:*

This is an incredible book! *FireBride* is filled with treasures to be mined by the body of Christ. It isn't the *milk* of the Word; it is *meat*. Be prepared for transformation as you enter these pages. No one can read this book without going on a spiritual journey.

—CINDY JACOBS, FOUNDING PRESIDENT
GENERALS OF INTERCESSION

A *powerful* book for *now*, written by one of the most *powerful* women of God I have ever known. You will feel the glory fire of the *FireBride!*

—DR. MARK HANBY, APOSTLE AND FOUNDER
MARK HANBY MINISTRIES

Must reading for every serious contender who desires to be a part of the bride of Christ. *FireBride* is an absorbing book that not only reveals *how* the Lord is preparing His bride for glory but also *why* He's chosen the unconditional fiery path He has. The author paints compelling word mosaics while presenting a consummate and prophetic portrait of what the glorious bride of Christ will *really* look like—and why.

—DORIS WAGNER, EXECUTIVE DIRECTOR
GLOBAL HARVEST MINISTRIES
(A.D. 2000 UNITED PRAYERTRACK)

FireBride presents a biblical foundation on which is built a clear prophetic insight into the "days of fire" before us. It challenges us to embrace the fire of God for our lives and the future of the church! A candid, clear, prophetic message to carry us through these last days.

—DR. BURT PURVIS, SENIOR PASTOR
THE CHURCH IN CITYVIEW

Margaret Moberly has been a dear friend for many years and is such a capable woman of God. She established a great organization for women ministers and has traveled extensively all over the world. Now she writes as a prophetess about the fire of God and how it puts us all to the test. You will enjoy reading from the soul of someone who writes so brilliantly and has been, and is, "there." Margaret Moberly's writing is beautiful!
—REV. MARILYNN GAZOWSKI, FOUNDING PASTOR
VOICE OF PENTECOST CHURCH

What a book! Margaret Moberly packs all of her intellect, deep spirituality and wisdom into the printed word and shares all of that in a book that needs to be in the personal library of every Spirit-filled believer. I unreservedly and strongly recommend her work across the broad spectrum of Christendom.
—REV. DR. LARRY W. BOGLE, PROFESSOR OF EDUCATION
SOUTHWESTERN ASSEMBLIES OF GOD UNIVERSITY

Conceived in great love and delivered in great joy, this marvelous work is meat for every hungry soul. It draws true biblical parallels from "The Glorious Fire of the God of Glory" to "The Glorious FireBride." A prophetic spiritual journey by way of the desert wilderness and along the Emmaus Road, *FireBride* defines how His church is being purified to come forth as pure gold, silver and precious stones. To Christ Jesus be all the praise!
—REVS. VERNON AND LINDA LOVE, FOUNDERS
MIDNIGHT HOUR MINISTRIES

FireBride

FireBride

Margaret Morgan Moberly

FIREBRIDE by Margaret Morgan Moberly
Published by Creation House
Strang Communications Company
600 Rinehart Road
Lake Mary, Florida 32746
www.creationhouse.com

Unless otherwise noted, all Scripture quotations are from the
New King James Version of the Bible. Copyright © 1979, 1980, 1982
by Thomas Nelson, Inc., publishers. Used by permission.

Scripture quotations marked AMP are from the Amplified Bible.
Old Testament copyright © 1965, 1987 by the Zondervan
Corporation. The Amplified New Testament copyright © 1954,
1958, 1987 by the Lockman Foundation. Used by permission.

Scripture quotations marked KJV are from the
King James Version of the Bible.

Library of Congress Cataloging-in-Publication Data

Moberly, Margaret Morgan.
Firebride/ by Margaret Morgan Moberly
p.   cm.
Includes bibliographical references.
ISBN 0-88419-589-9
1. Christian life—Biblical teaching.   2. Fire—Biblical teaching.
I. Title.
BS680.C47.M62 1999
243—dc21   98-45967
                                                           CIP

9 0 1 2 3 4 5 BBG 8 7 6 5 4 3 2 1

Printed in the United States of America

This book is dedicated to my wonderful husband, O. B., who has always been my unshakeable rock through every facet and stage of my life, second only to *the Rock* in magnitude and love. He has constantly been my greatest supporter, surest beacon and gentle protector, walking unselfishly always by my side. His steadfastness has been my surest provision, together with his unfailing love, gentle spirit and quiet wisdom. He has been my untiring helper and constant encourager, sustaining me throughout myriad endeavors, including the long and often difficult writing of this manuscript.

And so it is with immeasurable tenderness of spirit, together with an eternal and everlasting love for my beloved best friend that this book, along with my heart, is forever dedicated.

—MARGARET MORGAN MOBERLY

You found his heart faithful before You, and made a covenant with him.

—NEHEMIAH 9:8

The wisdom that is from above is first pure, then peaceable, gentle, willing to yield, full of mercy and good fruits.

—JAMES 3:17

Acknowledgments

It is with untold prayers and limitless love that I joyously acknowledge and give the Lord unending thanksgiving for every devoted friend and intercessor, both here and around the world, who have continually and with great faithfulness believed the promises of God to be made manifest in my life and for the writing of this book. You have not only continued to pray and believe with me, but you have been immovable through many days, months and years, always refusing to let go of the horns of the altar. You know who you are. Your spirit has identified with mine. More importantly, God knows and has always identified with you.

As faithful friends and the Lord's intercessors, the greatest and most enduring affirmation and loving acknowledgment I can give, of which you are so worthy, does not come from me, but sovereignly awaits you in His presence before the throne of grace. It is there for each of you that I will be daily petitioning Him to take my endless gratitude, highest love, ultimate prayers and greatest blessings and turn them into His greatest blessings for you in every aspect of your life.

And your Father who sees in secret will reward you openly.

—MATTHEW 6:6

For He Himself is our peace, who has made both one, and has broken down the middle wall of separation.

—Ephesians 2:14

Contents

Important Questions FireBride Answers

Chapter 1: The Glorious Fire of the God of Glory

- Why is it impossible for the glory of the bride to be conformed into His image without His consuming fire?
- What works of His are so essential to His plan that they must be secured and attained once again?
- How is He leading His people to accomplish His works now?
- What does it have to do with the impartation of His virtue and character?
- What one factor does He consider even more important than His essential power when it comes to being conformed into His image?

Chapter 2: Whose Fire Is This?

- What scriptural examples show us how both fires can operate concurrently?

- How are we able to know whose fire we're really in?
- How do we learn the critical difference between the enemy's fiery presence and God's fiery presence when both are committed to consuming the flesh?
- How do we escape the one while yielding to the other?

Chapter 3: The Fiery Armor of God

- Why is it not by accident that the verses dealing with God's armament are written to the Ephesian church rather than one of the other churches?
- Why is the Lord's strong admonishment in Revelation 2:4–5 written only to the church in Ephesus?
- Why is it an essential mandate that all of God's armor always be used without compromise?
- What makes God's fiery armor so vital to these last days?
- Why does Scripture assign such a precise sequence to how the armor is to be put on?

Chapter 4: The Great Shaking

- Who is responsible for this great shaking, and why?
- What can be done to lessen or escape its destructive impact?
- How can we recognize the truths concerning its purposes?
- What four things will remain standing after everything that can be shaken has been shaken?

Chapter 5: Fire Seasoned With Salt

- Why is the Salt Covenant more important now than at any other time in history?
- Why is fire absolutely necessary in the keeping of our Salt Covenant?
- What eight essential things does spiritual salt bring about in His body, and why?
- Why will the Lord receive no sacrifice from His people without His Salt Covenant?

Chapter 6: The Flaming Tongue

- Where and what is God's creative power source?
- When did He so designate it?
- Why did He decree His creative power source by the means and method He did?
- What is the one greatest and continuing conflict that rages daily in our lives?
- Why is the tongue the passageway to the spiritual world?

Chapter 7: The Road to Burning

- Where do we find the presence and the wisdom of God in these last days?
- How do we find the strength and ability to walk with Him continually?
- What does He say it takes to know Him intimately and faithfully?
- Why do we so quickly lose our focus in times of difficulty?
- What four essential spiritual principles must we learn if we are to be undefeated?

Chapter 8: The Blazing Desert Wilderness

- How will the final preparations of His FireBride be achieved?
- Why did Jesus lead them to Bethany and then leave them there?
- What things does He have to teach us in our own spiritual Bethany?
- Why would we not be able to learn them in any location other than Bethany?
- Why is the bride to make herself ready?
- How does the bride learn to overcome victoriously?

Chapter 9: The Glorious FireBride

- What nine things will the FireBride discover while learning to put her spiritual roots down ever deeper?
- What fifteen things will she know as she beholds His face, His ways and His voice that will cause Him to choose only her?
- What eighteen things has the bride been taught that will make her truly His glorious FireBride?

Foreword

This is an incredible book! The truths it contains are those that every Christian needs to learn in a deep way. *FireBride* is filled with treasures that should be mined by the body of Christ. It isn't the *milk* of the Word; it is *meat*.

I first met Margaret Moberly in 1982 while I lived in Weatherford, Texas. I was sinking in the depths of despair concerning my prophetic gifting. I didn't know what to do with it! She patiently took me by the hand and guided me out of the many messes I made and has been a mentor to me in my life.

Margaret has earned the right to teach on the fire of God. She was totally blind when she was a young girl, and God healed her. She has walked in the fire of the corporate world and supervised eighteen hundred employees. Through the years God has used her prophetic gift and wisdom both in the pulpit ministry and behind closed doors to teach and train His leaders.

The greatest glory fire came in her life in 1987 when she

suffered two strokes within twenty-four hours of each other, which damaged more than 50 percent of her brain. Since that time God has miraculously restored her mind and memory and, as evidenced by this book, her ability to communicate. Margaret Moberly has earned the right to write on this subject. She has lived it.

Not only has she experienced days of immeasurable pain without complaint, but she has also entered into a depth of intercession during this period of time that few understand.

Margaret is a great woman of God. She is my heroine. Please take time to read this book carefully. I have had to read it slowly and, at times, have read parts of it over and over.

Be prepared for transformation as you enter these pages. No one can read *FireBride* without going on a spiritual journey. I pray that God will use it in your life, as He has in mine, to burn off bondages and loose you into a measure of knowing Him you have never experienced before.

—CINDY JACOBS
GENERALS OF INTERCESSION
COLORADO SPRINGS, COLORADO

The sight of the glory of the LORD was like a consuming fire on the top of the mountain in the eyes of the children of Israel.

—Exodus 24:17

1

The Glorious Fire
of the God of Glory

God's Word still stands as the only unerring and irrefutable sentinel to all who would come to the door of revelation and knock.

In the last few years God's light of revelation has shone into areas of His Word that have remained sealed until the present time. Spiritual insights that have been previously hidden are being received, examined and understood through the Holy Spirit. What has been just as sovereign and apparent is the fact that these spiritual revelations by the Holy Spirit are increasingly and uncomfortably given at the expense of the church's previously held—and often currently held—traditions, beliefs, doctrines and ways.

In the last few years there has been a profusion of spiritual insights into where the body of Christ is at the present time and where it is going. Christians—laymen and leaders alike—have been focusing on what they believe is God's revealed plan for these last days.

The myriad exchanges of dialogue in shared perceptions,

considerations and convictions cover the entire spectrum—from small informal get-togethers with friends and family members to church study groups—in virtually every pulpit around the world. In addition there is a growing number of written materials—books, magazine articles and pamphlets—that are no less varied, divergent and extensive.

Collectively, all of these offerings present a continuing spiritual mosaic that portrays an abundance of revealed perceptions for the design and plan God is unfolding in these last days to prepare His church for glory. Yet in spite of all the ongoing spiritual revelations, a complete, well-defined picture of what awaits, and why, remains obscure, with many pieces still not fitting or silently missing.

However, the Lord continues to unveil additional pieces of the "Master's mystery puzzle" according to His own sovereign timetable and wisdom, often awaiting further prayer and intercession within that timetable before divulging another piece of His prophetic puzzle and how it fits.

In this age of increasing deceptions, the plumb line of God's Word must stand as never before as confirmation and verification of how He intends to manifest His glory in this His latter house and temple:

> "And I will shake all nations, and they shall come to the Desire of All Nations, and I will fill this temple [house] with glory," says the LORD of hosts. "The silver is Mine, and the gold is Mine," says the LORD of hosts. "The glory of this latter temple [house] shall be greater than the former," says the LORD of hosts.
> —HAGGAI 2:7–9

In a time of prayer the Lord spoke to my heart, saying, "Out of the world I called the nations. Out of those nations I have been calling the church. And now out of the church, I am at this hour calling My bride."

> And the Spirit and the bride say, "Come!" And let him who hears say, "Come!" And let him who thirsts come. Whoever desires, let him take of the water of life freely.
> —REVELATION 22:17

In these End Times, it is no longer an option to hear His voice. It has become essential not only to hear His voice *but also to know His ways*. Those Christians who are still unwilling to make that ultimate sacrifice of their flesh in an unrelenting submission to God are at risk through such waywardness of becoming too feeble and too weak to follow Him through the growing darkness that increasingly surrounds us.

> Wherefore lift up the hands which hang down, and the feeble knees; and make straight paths for your feet, lest that which is lame be turned out of the way; but let it rather be healed.
> —HEBREWS 12:12–13, KJV

> Strengthen the weak hands, and make firm the feeble knees. Say to those who are fearful-hearted, "Be strong, do not fear!"
> —ISAIAH 35:3–4

Today, God's Word and His Holy Spirit are our only sure compass. In times past there was enough spiritual daylight so that God could guide us by His pillar of cloud. Throughout those years we had enough light to make out the spiritual terrain and landmarks over which we were called upon to journey. But now, with the enemy's night of darkness growing rapidly around us with each step we take, it is God's pillar of fire that beckons us to follow closely.

The Lord's coming is imminent. Only by consistently seeking and following His pillar of fire will we be able to pursue Him closely and intimately enough to encounter the glory that is in that fiery presence. We will behold Him not only as Lord but also as Friend and Lover. Then His fiery light will not only radiate onto our darkened pathway but will, in turn, be reflected from us and onto a dark and dying world.

> Moreover You led them . . . by night with a pillar of fire, to give them light on the road which they should travel.
>
> —NEHEMIAH 9:12

> The night is far spent, the day is at hand. Therefore let us cast off the works of darkness, and let us put on the armor of light.
>
> —ROMANS 13:12

Those who are hungry for such a personal revival of God's glory are renewing and intensifying their commitment to prayer and intercession as He rekindles spiritual fires on a higher plane of fervency and urgency. Why? Because hearing His voice and knowing His ways have become more exacting—and profoundly more necessary—than ever before as the gross darkness of the enemy's night continues to escalate. (See John 9:4; Romans 13:12.)

Essentially, every committed Christian is seeking some vital answers to three fundamental questions as they endeavor to follow Him through the final hours of this dispensation:

- *What* are the last moves of His Spirit before He comes?
- *How long* will they last?
- And perhaps most important to our spiritual understanding: *Why* is He moving in this way?

In this book the Lord will walk us through *His* prophetic

scriptural answers to these questions—along with some of their innumerable facets—as He consummates the final maturing and perfecting of His FireBride.

For those who do not hunger and thirst after *scriptural* answers to these questions, this book may contain too many scriptures. However, for those who are once more fervently searching the Word of God for His fundamental, basic and vital answers to these questions, this book will prove fundamental.

And just in case there are Christians who have yet to notice, our God is taking us *all* not so quietly back once again to the very fundamental basics of His gospel. Through the years we have been searching for more of Jesus in an almost endless array of teaching precepts and methods. In the process we have obscured, and at times severely disfigured or lost, His simple ways and truths so vital to our walk.

We started out with the great beauty of His simplicity and have somehow ended up with great monumental complexities. The body of Christ has accumulated teaching upon teaching upon copious note-taking and taped soon-to-be-forgotten teaching at the expense of God's unchanging and fundamental basics of simplicity, clarity and truth.

> And they will turn their ears away from the truth.
> —2 TIMOTHY 4:4

> Nevertheless I have this against you, that you have left your first love. Remember therefore from where you have fallen; repent and do the first works.
> —REVELATION 2:4–5

In these chapters the church will encounter just what it is He *is* doing. We as His body may not be sure of many things, but the one thing we *are* sure of is that He will accomplish this final phase of His master plan in complete harmony with His infallible Word.

We are living on the last page of His blueprint, which He's been waiting to unfold since before the foundations of the world. In these last days and final hours He is revealing how He intends to fulfill that ultimate arrangement and plan. We know that with this phase of the Master's plan—as with every other phase—there will be no variation or shadow of turning from His Word:

> Every good gift and every perfect gift is from above, and comes down from the Father of lights, with whom there is no variation or shadow of turning.
> —JAMES 1:17

But still the questions remain:

- What *is* He doing?
- What works of His are so essential to His plan that they must be secured again in our lives before we can proceed to the ultimate level of His master plan?
- What is that final level, and how is He leading us to it and through it?
- What does it have to do—if anything—with an impartation into our lives of His virtue and character?
- What is it that He considers more important than even His essential power when it comes to being conformed and transformed into His image?
- Why does He so consider it?

> For whom He foreknew, He also predestined to be conformed to the image of His Son, that He might be the firstborn among many brethren.
> —ROMANS 8:29

Being conformed into God's image has always required a yielded vessel, molded by His character and by the fruit of His Spirit through which His power could purely flow. He is calling upon His church to be thoroughly weighed as He tempers His spiritual nature into her, imparting of:

- His fruit and His character.
- His anointing.
- His power.
- His glory.

There is little doubt that this is the order God intends for each of us, since it is the one set forth by His Son as our example. Before the anointing, power and glory were imparted in ultimate and fullest measure, the Father's love esteemed it necessary that His Son be tested by His Word in the wilderness (Matt. 4:1–11).

Jesus is presently about the business of showing us the need to reprioritize our spiritual lives in order to secure His Word again as the foremost foundation of our lives.

He is no longer making allowances for any skipped spiritual bases or failed testings along the way of reestablishing His first work bases. We somehow became so enamored with His power and power gifts that we have either missed or forgotten the enormity that He has unchangeably placed on those first works.

They will produce God's spiritual environment, compelling us to fully develop the character of Christ. Now we are finding out how much we have needed those basic first works, and we are finding how much we need their resultant stability as we strive to finish the race.

As to the "Why are You doing it, Lord?" we will look into His unmistakable answers as to why He would choose the way He has chosen in order to prepare and equip us for total and glorious victory.

Why did He choose such precise and exacting ways?

And why would our obtaining—and then living—this same exact spiritual sequence of His ascendancy be indispensable for becoming a partaker of that same glorious divine nature?

Why is it so uncompromisingly necessary before His glory can be fully manifested in us?

Why do we always seem to run into His constraints, which limit us as we attempt to receive His anointing and then to impart it to others?

We will scripturally meet the answers to these questions throughout the pages of this book. But a hint of one of His first answers should become visible with the following two scriptures:

> By which have been given to us exceedingly great and precious promises, that through these you may be partakers of the divine nature, having escaped the corruption that is in the world through lust.
>
> —2 PETER 1:4

> Do all things without complaining and disputing, that you may become blameless and harmless, children of God without fault in the midst of a crooked and perverse generation, among whom you shine as lights in the world.
>
> —PHILIPPIANS 2:14–15

As for the question, "When will You do it, Lord?" His time frame is from now until we see Him face to face. He is doing it now.

> For now we see in a mirror, dimly, but then face to face. Now I know in part, but then I shall know just as I also am known.
>
> —1 CORINTHIANS 13:12

> And this gospel of the kingdom will be preached in all
> the world as a witness to all the nations, and then the
> end will come.
>
> —MATTHEW 24:14

Lastly, and most importantly, "How will You do it,
Lord?"

How He will do it is the principal motivation for this
work. He will do it by the release of God's holy, consuming
glory fire into every aspect of our lives as He refines,
purges and purifies His beloved bride as gold, silver and
precious stones.

He will do it by His glory fire burning off all of our chaff
from His grain, and then sowing that grain beside all
waters to reap a mighty harvest of thirtyfold, sixtyfold and
a hundredfold for His glory.

He will do it by being who He is: a consuming fire.

> For the LORD your God is a consuming fire.
>
> —DEUTERONOMY 4:24

> For our God is a consuming fire.
>
> —HEBREWS 12:29

> But He who is coming after me . . . will baptize you
> with the Holy Spirit and with fire . . . and He will
> thoroughly clean out His threshing floor, and gather
> His wheat into the barn; but He will burn up the chaff
> with unquenchable fire.
>
> —MATTHEW 3:11–12

Fifty-three times in God's plan for the tabernacle and
temple throughout Scripture He commands the offerings
that were to be received and accepted by Him to be an
"offering made by fire." Just as Jesus' life became the actual
substance for the shadow and type of that tabernacle plan,
so we as His body are still fulfilling God's transcendent

plan revealed in Romans 8:29—that Jesus Christ was to become the firstborn of many brethren.

He purely and completely fulfilled God's will, and along with the power of His Holy Spirit, He left us with the perfected pattern, to be conformed and transformed into that same image. He consistently illustrated God's eternal life-giving principles, and then exclaimed, "I am the light of the world" (John 8:12). Having imparted His life into those who would follow Him, He then turned around and proclaimed, "You are the light of the world" (Matt. 5:14).

> Do you not know that you are the temple of God? . . . Or do you not know that your body is the temple of the Holy Spirit who is in you, whom you have from God, and you are not your own?
> —1 CORINTHIANS 3:16; 6:19

> Now, therefore, you are no longer strangers and foreigners, but fellow citizens with the saints and members of the household of God, having been built on the foundation of the apostles and prophets, Jesus Christ Himself being the chief cornerstone, in whom the whole building, being fitted together, grows into a holy temple in the Lord, in whom you also are being built together for a dwelling place of God in the Spirit.
> —EPHESIANS 2:19–22

When setting forth His charge to His priests, over thirty times in the Scriptures God had commanded that every sacrifice placed on the altar of sacrifice was to be offered solely and received solely by means of a consuming fire. That fire was the natural manifestation that symbolized God's spiritual operation as a consuming fire.

Always remember this spiritual principle: For every spiritual operation in the kingdom of God there will be a natural manifestation. When we operate in and by the

Holy Spirit, the Lord will never leave us out in some ethereal never-never land without some natural manifestation as evidence and confirmation that what we are doing is truly of Him.

If I tell you that Jesus personally came to me and imparted His love anointing to me, and yet show you no greater love as the natural manifestation of that spiritual visitation, then I'm either lying or I've been deceived. Either way that spiritual operation was not of God. Without exception, for every spiritual operation there will be a natural manifestation. We truly do have a very precise, sensible, orderly God!

We are fulfilling that same principle when we implement our priestly charge to offer up spiritual sacrifices that we have patterned after and inherited from our High Priest. Throughout Scripture sacrifices have been received by means of that consuming fire, described by God in both the Old and New Testaments as "a sweet-smelling savor" and "a sweet-smelling fragrance." It remains today as a precious prerequisite and His unequaled sign of how thoroughly and unconditionally He honors and receives the sacrifice.

Our Lord is the same yesterday, today and forever. Yet too many of us will quickly disregard the fact that God is still a consuming fire. Erroneous perceptions and interpretations of the Old Testament God continue to die hard—those of a cruel and ruthless God, eternally enraged, standing over His people with a great cosmic club mercilessly waiting to punish. Today these lying perceptions still remain as one of the biggest subterfuges that Satan ever perpetrated on God's people. In addition to this, there is the rebellious and carnal flesh—Satan's always-present cohort—constantly embellishing the great lie with its self-protecting rationale. Flesh will always believe it can be godly without having to deny and crucify its own desires and ways.

Could it be that we have not *yet* understood one of the greatest and most paradoxical spiritual truths in our lives? We are walking with a God who really is a consuming fire while simultaneously being consummate love!

That is the ultimate enigma of our God. He is a God who is eternally and unchangingly a consuming fire; at the same time He is perfect and eternal love. These four words—*consuming fire, consummate love*—do more than describe two characteristics and attributes of God. Scripture tells us they are the very essence of who and what God is (Heb. 12:29; 1 John 4:8).

Does it not then follow that God's consuming fire is also one of consummate love?

Does it not follow as well that such a consuming fire will *never* destroy even one of our precious promises for which He died?

And does it not also follow that He will consume *everything* that is not of Him that stands in the way of His ultimate best and highest good for us in fulfilling those promises?

> And the Angel of the LORD appeared to him in a flame of fire from the midst of a bush. So he looked, and behold, the bush was burning with fire, but the bush was not consumed. Then Moses said, "I will turn aside and see this great sight, why the bush does not burn."
> —EXODUS 3:2–3

Did we not cast three men bound into the midst of the fire? . . . I see four men loose, walking in the midst of the fire; and they are not hurt, and the form of the fourth is like the Son of God.

—DANIEL 3:24–25

2

Whose Fire Is This?

Shadrach, Meshach and Abednego knew whose fire they were in. Their belief in their God's love was as absolute as their faith. They knew whose consuming fire was in faultless control. From a small child each had been taught that their God was a consuming fire.

They went into the enemy's fire with their very lives ordered on that belief. They knew that He alone was in control of how long and how hot any enemy's fiery presence—*for His purposes*—would be allowed to burn into any situation or circumstance. From the record of the time when Moses first saw the fiery mountain and beheld the *glory* of God as a *fire* that perpetually burns, they knew that nothing that is of Him is ever consumed (Exod. 3:2).

> Surely the LORD our God has shown us His glory and His greatness, and we have heard His voice from the midst of the fire.
>
> —DEUTERONOMY 5:24

His throne was a fiery flame, its wheels a burning fire;
a fiery stream issued and came forth from before Him.
A thousand thousands ministered to Him.
—DANIEL 7:9–10

Every element of our lives that is *of Him*—every circumstance, event, deed, word and attitude given in trust and faith to Him—will never be consumed in any fire. At the same time all those things that are not wholly of Him will be either purged, refined or consumed.

Today as never before, the Lord is appearing in the midst of lives as a consuming fire. He is a pillar of fire to all who desire to come closer, hungering after His voice, His ways and His glory. And just as surely, He is appearing as that same consuming fire to those who do not choose to be involved with a closer walk.

But who can endure the day of His coming? And who can stand when He appears? For He is like a refiner's fire and like launderers' soap. He will sit as a refiner and a purifier of silver; He will purify the sons of Levi, and purge them as gold and silver, that they may offer to the LORD an offering in righteousness.
—MALACHI 3:2–3

When the children of Israel presented their offerings on the altar of sacrifice to God, He commanded that the sacrifice be offered by means of a consuming fire. Have we lost sight of the fact that since Calvary enemy fires have no control or authority over our lives, unless we yield some portion of our lives to Satan and will not repent?

Do you not know that to whom you present yourselves slaves to obey, you are that one's slaves whom you obey, whether of sin leading to death, or of obedience leading to righteousness?
—ROMANS 6:16

Suffice it to say that we find ourselves in many circumstances and situations where we yield our members to serve the flesh or Satan in some capacity. In fact, if we have not found ourselves far too frequently in such dark miry pits, a reality check needs to be taken for candor and safeguards against deceptions!

Whatever the situations of the past, our focus has often centered on rebel fires. These fires may be the flaming fires of our own fleshy will and desires that have not been daily crucified with Christ. Or they may be fires of satanic warfare by principalities, powers, rulers of darkness and spiritual wickedness in high places (Eph. 6:12). For most of us, however, it is usually a combination of the two.

Enemy fires are a hated but excellent incentive for checking the condition of our warfare weapons. They cause us to prayerfully search our hearts, repent, forgive and become stronger and less vulnerable to future attacks as a result of what we have learned in previous ones. In short, *God uses the enemy for His own purposes* in warfare aptitude testing! The triumphant result is that there is less flesh for the enemy to attack and more of God to fight and secure complete victory.

> For the ruler of this world is coming, and he has nothing in Me.
>
> —JOHN 14:30

> For you died, and your life is hidden with Christ in God.
>
> —COLOSSIANS 3:3

The problem with the body of Christ is that we have multitudinous occasions where our flesh, alive and well, sticks out from the altar of sacrifice, exposing where we are! But when we become dead to everything except Jesus Christ, the enemy will find nothing in us that is not of Him.

It has become a growing necessity to understand whose fire we are really in *and why*. As never before, God is calling His body to focus spiritual eyes intensely and fervently on Him alone. When we are able to do that, we will recognize that no matter how hot and intense the fire is, He will *only* allow those things that are obstacles and hindrances to our being conformed into His image to be consumed.

WE'RE IN THE GLORY FIRE!

> I beseech you therefore, brethren, by the mercies of God, that you present your bodies a living sacrifice, holy, acceptable to God, which is your reasonable service.
> —ROMANS 12:1

In presenting our bodies as a living sacrifice, in the past we have had a strong tendency to get up quietly and walk off the altar when the fires became too intense. The flesh was not dead enough in some particular area, and it became too painful to stay on the altar.

However, He loves us enough that in these End Times we are no longer going to be able to retain such death-defying capabilities of the flesh or will. He is teaching us how to walk through every darkness by His Spirit and pillar of fire alone, by *staying on* the altar of sacrifice. These fiery testings, trials and temptations will continue to increase until we see Him face to face—*as will the increased victories in Him* (2 Tim. 3:13; Isa. 60:2).

The Lord in His love is allowing us to see how crucial it is that we keep our spiritual, emotional and mental eyes upon Him, regardless of the trial, testing or circumstance—totally and completely on Him, *regardless*. It is no longer an option; only deception ever said it was. He is no longer winking at our relapses and regressions when we willfully climb down off His sacrificial altar as the fires are heated seven times hotter.

Truly, these times of ignorance God overlooked [winked at], but now commands all men everywhere to repent.

—ACTS 17:30

No temptation has overtaken you except such as is common to man; but God is faithful, who will not allow you to be tempted beyond what you are able, but with the temptation will also make the way of escape, that you may be able to bear it.

—1 CORINTHIANS 10:13

The Lord is preparing an overcoming church, a mature bride. One who no longer follows after Him in childish shallowness, asking for "recess time" or "time out" when she tires of His righteous standards for a sacrificial life wholly separated unto Him. One who is *childlike* in trust, faith and humility—but no longer *childish*.

If anyone desires to come after Me, let him deny himself, and take up his cross, and follow Me. For whoever desires to save his life will lose it, but whoever loses his life for My sake will find it.

—MATTHEW 16:24–25

Our explanations for crawling off the altar have been without number. Along the way there have been fears, hurts, weariness, pride, disappointments, unforgiveness, discouragements, vanity, hopelessness, lusts and others.

However, God loves us too much to accept even the worst of sins or the best of rationales as justification for lack of fervency, intensity and total commitment. He is in the process of seeing to it that our flesh *will* die regardless of the reasons. Paradoxically, the *only* safe place for us is on the altar in the midst of His fire.

There are two spiritual beings after our radical demise. One is Satan; the other is God. Carnal flesh will end up in total destruction by one or the other.

His holy, consuming fire of glory is burning off all the chaff and removing all the dross in order to shape and manifest His divine character into our transformed lives. As the impurities and contaminants are being purged, purifying our hearts and lives, we realize this has been His divine plan for perfecting His bride from the beginning.

This is the fiery process whereby all the yokes and bondages are burned off. No smell of smoke remains around the radiance of His bride. It is the only way found in His Word whereby He produces His vessels of mercy— as well as His gold.

Throughout the centuries it has been said that the molding of the original golden candlesticks in the wilderness tabernacle has never been duplicated. All seven branches that came out from the main branch were intricately and ornately fashioned from just one seamless piece of pure gold. Only by allowing God's Spirit to take control of his mind, hands and spirit was the craftsman, named Bezalel, able to fulfill God's instructions and achieve such a seemingly impossible work.

> See, I have called by name Bezalel . . . of the tribe of Judah. And I have filled him with the Spirit of God, in wisdom, in understanding, in knowledge, and in all manner of workmanship.
>
> —Exodus 31:2–3

It was believed that the goldsmith refined and shaped the gold for the candlestick by placing each stage of the work in fires having progressively hotter temperatures. The temperature for each heating of the precious metal was painstakingly timed and watched over. Too hot for too long and the design would be lost. Not hot enough or not long enough and it would remain too brittle and inflexible for the next stage of fashioning.

Each time the precious metal was removed from the fire, it was more pliable—ready for the next stage required to mold each exquisite detail of God's final design. The precious gold would be removed from the fire long enough for resting and cooling, then with that precision timing known only to God and Bezalel, the master craftsman, it would be ready for the next stage of the fiery process after testing its resistance, pliability and flexibility.

God had given the goldsmith alone the wisdom to know the exact degree of temperature required for each stage and its precise timing. He alone held the ability to accomplish the work. He alone had the ability to envision how the priceless treasure was to look when finished. Again and again, he would let each stage have its fiery work on the precious metal under his hands, allowing the fire's intensities to create the needed yieldedness to transform the gold into a one-of-a-kind work of art.

The original was so transparent that not only was it the vessel that *held* God's light, it actually appeared to have *become* that light, completely illuminating the holy place.

Now we can see why such exquisite care was taken to fashion the original tabernacle's golden candlestick and why it was never duplicated. As His body on earth, we are now following the same pattern that Jesus followed as God's original gold lampstand holding God's light.

The name *Bezalel* in Hebrew means "in the shadow of the protection of the Almighty." As His tabernacle, the bride, who is always in the shadow of His wings and under the protection of the Almighty, is being fashioned as a faithful replica of God's lampstand and as the light of the world. We are continually being forged in the glory fire by the Master Craftsman to hold His light with such transparency that nothing but the glory of God through Jesus Christ will shine through.

He is saying, "Come, My beloved, hold My hand and don't lose sight of My love or My face. We are going to mold this area of your life now, together with this portion of your character, and purge this expanse of My precious gold of more dross."

> Beloved, do not think it strange concerning the fiery trial which is to try you, as though some strange thing happened to you; but *rejoice* to the extent that you partake of Christ's sufferings, that when His glory is revealed, you may also be glad with exceeding joy.
> —1 PETER 4:12–13, EMPHASIS ADDED

In the time that remains before His coming, it has become crucial to know and remember whose fire has ultimate control over our lives. God is speaking loud and clear, reminding us that it is *not* the enemy's fire. He will continue to unsheathe the sword of His Word by the Scriptures and the Holy Spirit to give us ever-increasing knowledge, understanding and revelation. And one of the principal ways this will be achieved is by the escalation of our walk through fiery places.

These are times when He continues to open the eyes of our understanding to the reality that it is "the fourth man" who is walking with us in the midst of our fiery temptations, testings and trials. He still is retaining absolute dominion, power and authority over each phase.

It is perhaps most perfectly and flawlessly summed up in just one sentence by Joseph in the Book of Genesis. He spoke revelation knowledge by the Spirit regarding all the years of continuous and extraordinary evil through which he had lived:

> But as for you [the flesh and Satan], you meant evil against me; but God meant it for good.
> —GENESIS 50:20

God would give a striking double enunciation of this

eternal, pivotal truth through Paul when writing to all who
were to come afterward in the Lord's new dispensation of
the New Testament Blood Covenant.

> And we know that all things work together for good
> to those who love God, to those who are the called
> according to His purpose.
> —ROMANS 8:28

The same fiery trials . . . the same fiery circumstances . . . the same fiery testings . . . just like the three
Hebrew children, Joseph and Paul, who came to *know*
whose *ultimate* fire they were in:

> He [Joseph] was laid in irons. Until the time that his
> word came to pass, the word of the LORD tested him.
> —PSALM 105:18–19

That is the key. We are being established in the midst of
God's glory fire, which burns off everything in us that *is not
of Him* by strengthening and tempering everything in us
that *is of Him*.

That leaves the essential question of how we yield to
God's glory fire while still withstanding the enemy's fire.
The answer, another of His paradoxes, is a fundamental of
the gospel to which the Lord is bringing us back. We do so
by walking on in Him as we fight the enemy with God's
promises, steadfastly and unshakeably standing on the solid
foundation of the Rock with our eyes fixed on the Author
and Finisher of our faith.

The bride can no longer allow her steps to vacillate or to
veer from God's Word and His promises onto the enemy's
shifting sands of pride, doubt, wounds and fear. But isn't
that extremely difficult? No. It is quite *impossible* without
His being with us, in us, through us and around us with
every step we take.

> For in Him we live and move and have our being, as
> also some of your own poets have said, "For we are
> also His offspring."
>
> —ACTS 17:28

> Therefore whoever hears these sayings of Mine, and
> does them, I will liken him to a wise man who built his
> house on the rock: and the rain descended, the floods
> came, and the winds blew and beat on that house; and
> it did not fall, for it was founded on the rock. But
> everyone who hears these sayings of Mine, and does
> not do them, will be like a foolish man who built his
> house on the sand: and the rain descended, the floods
> came, and the winds blew and beat on that house; and
> it fell. And great was its fall.
>
> —MATTHEW 7:24–27

We will yield to God's glory and withstand the enemy's
fire by enlarging our understanding and strengthening our
trust and faith while continuing to build *only* on the Rock's
basic foundational principles. We must hold *steadfast*, literally through all the hell of the enemy's counterfeit fires,
even when those fires are heated up seven times hotter.

We have perhaps lost sight of another fundamental
truth. God is the *only One* who can create. Satan remains
the deadly and dazzling counterfeiter who cannot originate
anything, including fires. In these End Times we need to
understand that. He is only able to come up with the most
hellish counterfeit, which is still under ultimate subjection
to the Original:

> "Behold, I have created the blacksmith [and gold-
> smith] who blows the coals in the fire, who brings
> forth an instrument for his work; and I have created
> the spoiler to destroy. No weapon formed against you
> shall prosper, and every tongue which rises against
> you in judgment you shall condemn. This is the her-

itage of the servants of the LORD, and their righteousness is from Me," says the LORD.

—ISAIAH 54:16–17

Our Lord is in the process of so purging our lives with His glory fire that what remains is becoming a clear, pure, unrestricted channel through which His anointed character and power can freely flow. Nothing to restrict it . . . nothing to diminish it . . . nothing of the flesh to catch it . . . nothing of the enemy to seize and bind it . . . no distortion to dam it. . . . As His bride we are becoming that transparent, radiant vessel who will purely reflect His shining glory.

Throughout the body of Christ we have become most proficient in the practice of fighting many aspects of enemy warfare. To put it in the shortest possible summation, the body of Christ has been majoring on all the ravages of the devil's fires. There should be no doubt that setting the captives free and bringing deliverance from all forms of enemy bondages should and will continue as one of God's priorities from now until we see Him face to face.

> The Spirit of the LORD is upon Me, because He has anointed Me to preach the gospel to the poor; He has sent Me to heal the brokenhearted, to proclaim liberty to the captives and recovery of sight to the blind, to set at liberty those who are oppressed.
>
> —LUKE 4:18

Have not we in the body of Christ too many times fought enemy fires, disregarding the truth that Satan's counterfeit fires are subject to God's original fire of glory? Jesus came to destroy the works of the devil. But He did it by keeping His eyes exclusively on the Father, doing only what He saw the Father doing and saying only what He heard the Father saying. He did not accomplish it by keeping His eyes on the enemy and the works of the devil.

When our spiritual eyes and ears are kept unshakeably upon the Lord, He will give us His strategy as well as His weapons to destroy all the fiery works of the enemy, and He will give us complete victory. But if we are unwilling to maintain that steadfast focus, with eyes single on the Lord, we will be caught up again and again in a spiraling, swirling vortex of fleshly or spiritual counterfeits, with emotions and reactions that the enemy can use for our destruction.

We have become ensnared too many times by our own *reactions*, rather than find God's plan of *action*. Such reactions have made hearing His voice not only more difficult, but too often impossible. Learning to *respond* and *act*—rather than *react*—to *only* what God has spoken and shown us is a spiritual assignment He has had us majoring on for some time. Is there anyone who has not yet noticed?

We are now being given our final exams. Though they may seem extremely difficult, He does not give them without already knowing His bride's ability in Him to pass them with flying colors and the banner of victory. Why? Because His bride will seek Him as *Jehovah-Nissi*, our banner and our victory.

In working through the difficult lessons for these finals, many of us are finding out that most of the answers are the same ones He has been teaching us over and over and over again. These answers consist simply of not being stunned, shaken or frightened into reacting to any of the fiery attacks of the enemy. We are finding that the more fiery the attacks, the more absolute the necessity that these lessons be learned. We are also finding that it is as difficult as it is necessary.

However, God's assignments and final exams are spiritual prerequisites to be secured if we are to continue to live victoriously in Him until He comes. We cannot afford to lose sight of whose fire is in control, regardless of the heat of the battles.

If we can keep that unshakeable fact within our focus—

no matter how intense and frequent the enemy's fiery attacks—then each fiery test, trial and temptation will only serve to fashion and temper more of God's fruit of the Spirit in us. The fruit is His character—as well as His honor, His power and His victory. He is releasing more of His fiery light of glory into our lives. It burns brightly and more steadfastly in us, reaching out to a lost and dying world.

We will continue to walk in fiery places. That is why Peter exhorts us not to think it strange when another fiery trial hits us, because it will. The Lord says to *rejoice*, because we know whose ultimate fire we are in. We know what is being burned off. It is everything in us that cannot be used in the kingdom of God, whatever is a hindrance to us in our own lives.

He is equipping us to yield to His glory fire and to be able to say, "Lord, I want to be a sweet-smelling savor to you. I don't want to come out of this smelling of smoke or with any bonds or yokes left anywhere around me or on me."

In these last days we cannot afford to ignore the lessons taught by the Lord's use of King Nebuchanezzar's fiery furnace whenever we are tempted to believe that our fiery testings and trials are under the dictates of the enemy.

The king thought the fate of the three Israelite boys was totally in his hands: "And who is the god who will deliver you from my hands?" (Dan. 3:15). But the important question is: In whose hand is the enemy? The three Hebrew children knew that the enemy is always in God's hands—just as they knew they were always in His hands.

We will not be under the sway or influence of enemy fires if we know to whom we have yielded our members. We will know whose we are. And God knows whose we are: "Neither shall anyone snatch them out of My hand" (John 10:28).

We are living in a day and time when everything that can be shaken is being shaken:

But now He has promised, saying, "Yet once more I shake not only the earth, but also heaven." Now this, "Yet once more," indicates the removal of those things that are being shaken, as of things that are made, that the things which cannot be shaken may remain. Therefore, since we are receiving a kingdom which cannot be shaken, let us have grace, by which we may serve God acceptably with reverence and godly fear. *For our God is a consuming fire.*
—HEBREWS 12:26–29, EMPHASIS ADDED

When we walk in the midst of that fire, the Lord is teaching us to rejoice just as the early church did. He is still consuming all that is not of Him as we walk with, and in, His glorious fiery presence—everything that would create a stumbling block to becoming more like Him. That means all of the weights, all of the yokes, all of the bondages, all of the impurities. In short, all of the wood, hay and stubble in our lives. These are the days in which He is trying every man's work with His consuming glory fire.

For other foundation can no man lay than that is laid, which is Jesus Christ. Now if any man build upon this foundation gold, silver, precious stones, wood, hay, stubble; every man's work shall be made manifest: for the day shall declare it, because it shall be revealed by fire; and the fire shall try every man's work of what sort it is.
—1 CORINTHIANS 3:11–13, KJV

That the trial of your faith, being much more precious than of gold that perisheth, though it be tried with fire, might be found unto praise and honour and glory at the appearing of Jesus Christ.
—1 PETER 1:7, KJV

What is going to be left after the glory fire? Each one of

us will be left as His very own beloved precious gold, His beloved FireBride of glory. We are walking with Him and in Him in the midst of that glorious fire, allowing the Spirit to fashion the Lord's priceless gold and silver dove. As His bride, we are that cherished dove described in the Book of Psalms and the Song of Solomon:

> Though you lie down among the sheepfolds, you will be like the wings of a dove covered with silver, and her feathers with yellow gold.
> —PSALM 68:13

> O my dove, in the clefts of the rock...
> —SONG OF SOLOMON 2:14

> Open for me, my sister, my love, my dove, my perfect one.
> —SONG OF SOLOMON 5:2

> My dove, my perfect one, is the only one.
> —SONG OF SOLOMON 6:9

The early church had been thoroughly introduced to the Lord's teachings of truth principles by means of paradoxes and dichotomies. By both revelation and illustration, Jesus taught that God's purposes are a deliberate antithesis to man's ways.

Because God understood His fallen creation so intrinsically, He knew that carnal man, when left to his own will, devices and pride, would invariably become presumptuous enough to touch His glory. Consequently, scriptural examples are replete from Genesis to Revelation, illustrating God's infinite wisdom in His use of sovereign antitheses for the fulfillment of His will and purposes. These antitheses include:

- The garment of praise for heaviness.
- Joy in the midst of suffering.
- Plenty in the midst of want.
- Life for death.
- Beauty for ashes.

These are but five tip-of-the-iceberg principles from an almost endless number in Scripture. God longs to impart a greater degree of spiritual understanding to this His latter church than was imparted to the early church. However, His paradoxes and parables have remained obscured today much as they were when He first walked on His earth. Too few yet perceive their meanings.

> Therefore I speak to them in parables, because seeing they do not see, and hearing they do not hear, nor do they understand. And in them the prophecy of Isaiah is fulfilled, which says: "Hearing you will hear and shall not understand, and seeing you will see and not perceive; for the hearts of this people have grown dull. Their ears are hard of hearing, and their eyes they have closed, lest they should see with their eyes and hear with their ears, lest they should understand with their hearts and turn, so that I should heal them."
> —MATTHEW 13:13–15

> When anyone hears the word of the kingdom, and does not understand it, then the wicked one comes and snatches what was sown in his heart.
> —MATTHEW 13:19

> When He had called the multitude to Himself, He said to them, "Hear and understand."
> —MATTHEW 15:10

Over twenty-eight times in the Gospels, as He spoke

and taught Jesus exhorted His disciples, as well as the multitudes, that it was imperative that they not only hear, but understand. That they not only look, but perceive. The fact that they still did not understand or perceive seemed to elicit one of our Lord's most frequent and deeply felt emotions, reflecting His pain and grief over the desperate state of fallen man with his darkened perceptions.

Again and again He would say to His disciples:

> Do you not yet understand?
>   —MATTHEW 15:17

> How is it you do not understand?
>   —MATTHEW 16:11

He ultimately answered that last question for them Himself:

> It is the Spirit who gives life; the flesh profits nothing. The words that I speak to you are spirit, and they are life.
>   —JOHN 6:63

Paul echoed and amplified that essential spiritual principle when writing to the Corinthians:

> These things we also speak, not in words which man's wisdom teaches but which the Holy Spirit teaches, comparing spiritual things with spiritual. But the natural man does not receive the things of the Spirit of God, for they are foolishness to him; nor can he know them, because they are [only] spiritually discerned.
>   —1 CORINTHIANS 2:13–14

The Lord is taking us all inexorably back to the fundamental simplicity of the Gospels one last time, to the place

31

where Jesus sat down on a hillside and taught in ways that even the most unlearned of men could perceive the eternal, unchanging truths and ways of God. The only requirement is a hungry and thirsty heart. And that is still His only requirement today—*a hungry and thirsty heart*. He is taking us back one more time to hear Him say:

> You are mistaken, not knowing the Scriptures nor the power of God.
> —MATTHEW 22:29; CF. MARK 12:24

Through Paul, we are being brought back one last time to the Lord's warning for these End Times. And this warning is probably more vital today than at any other time in Christian history:

> But I fear, lest by any means, as the serpent beguiled Eve through his subtilty [craftiness], so your minds should be corrupted from the simplicity that is in Christ.
> —2 CORINTHIANS 11:3, KJV

We are being brought back afresh and anew to the simplicity of Jesus, the Word made flesh.

> You search the Scriptures, for in them you think you have eternal life; and these are they which testify of Me.
> —JOHN 5:39

Perhaps most importantly of all, we are being brought back anew and afresh in these last days to God's firm, unshakeable foundation, enabling us to remove the deceptive scales from over our eyes and ears that were formed by the perpetual pursuit of spiritual complexities. Such complexities have taken us far afield from the simplicity of His never-changing plumb line of His ways and Word. Once again He is revealing God's unshakeable foundation of simplicity to answer what God is doing—and why and how—as we follow His pillar of fire to glory.

> That you may approve the things that are excellent, that you may be sincere and without offense till the day of Christ, being filled with fruits of righteousness which are by Jesus Christ, to the glory and praise of God.
>
> —PHILIPPIANS 1:10–11

Finally, my brethren, be strong in the Lord and in the power of His might. Put on the whole armor of God, that you may be able to stand against the wiles of the devil.

—Ephesians 6:10–11

3

The Fiery Armor of God

Firefighters have discovered how to fight the most dangerous and devastating of fires, which endanger their own lives as well as the territory and terrain that they are fighting to protect. They have achieved successful victories by setting a fire wall of their own creation to fight the enemy fires.

They understand God's natural laws enough to know that their own consuming blaze would confront the attacking fires, extinguishing and destroying them at their fiery source. They realize that victory can be achieved by using offensive fire strategies rather than merely fighting defensively.

Knowingly or unknowingly, they have uncovered a significant and important spiritual principle: The Lord fights the fiery attacks of the enemy offensively by simply being who He is—*a consuming fire*.

We have already established the fact that for every spiritual operation there will *always* be a natural manifestation.

While the natural manifestation is evident from natural fires with natural firefighters, the Lord's children have been a great deal slower in learning that the original *spiritual* source of that operation is God's consuming fire.

Certainly this spiritual principle emerges and begs to be addressed if we are to gain discernment in fighting the enemy's fires equipped with God's armor. That armor was forged out of the fires of His very essence as a consuming fire. Each weapon has been fashioned by God Himself and shaped in the all-consuming fires of His glory.

Every piece that was fashioned for us from His fiery essence had to be purchased by His Son with His baptism of fire. It is the armor that had been promised, guaranteed, witnessed and sealed by that fiery cross of His blood covenant. This fiery armor will defeat all attacks of the enemy, whether that enemy is our flesh or Satan. It is the fiery armor of God Almighty, and it will consume anything that is not of Him.

> Under his glory he will kindle a burning like the burning of a fire. So the Light of Israel will be for a fire, and His Holy One for a flame; it will burn and devour his thorns and his briers in one day.
> —Isaiah 10:16–17

Jesus Christ alone paid the price for the forging of our armament in the consuming fires of a holy God. His armor becomes a tempering fire as well as a protective fire to every Christian who puts it on. Simultaneously, it becomes a disastrous fire to the enemy whenever and wherever he encounters it—whether that enemy is our flesh or Satan. We have not yet begun to comprehend what God's armor is and its priceless worth and significance.

Is there one of us who has not quoted the seven verses from Ephesians 6:12–18 concerning God's armor with all of the spiritual depth and interest of reciting a Sunday school memory verse? This is where many first learned of them, complete with the little song and gestures that went along with them.

Even after these scriptures have been exercised, there still remains a great tendency to recount them by rote from the mind and not from the heart and spirit. Perhaps that is because we have not yet *really* understood how essential they are to our lives in this End Time.

Whatever the reason, Christians continue to be exposed needlessly in battle, jeopardizing too many victories. There is a vital urgency to develop a greater understanding and perception of the design, function and purpose of God's armor. Too many of us have allowed time and familiarity to erode whatever weight God's armor once occupied in our lives. The Lord is bringing His church back to this critical foundational first work also.

Now is the time when God is about His priority business of His healing restoration and fiery renewal of His body. He is achieving it by bringing us all back to the pure, unfeigned simplicity of His ways. He is achieving it by pronouncing the truth that we have left our first love and need to do our first works over again, much as He spelled it out to the Ephesian church:

> Nevertheless I have this against you, that you have left your first love. Remember therefore from where you have fallen; repent and do the first works, or else I will come to you quickly and remove your lampstand from its place—unless you repent.
>
> —REVELATION 2:4–5

Is it just a coincidence that the seven verses dealing with God's armament came from the Book of Ephesians?

Is just a coincidence that these verses in Revelation were written as an admonishment to the Ephesian church?

Could it be that this was a part of their first works,

which, when left, caused them to leave their first love?

Jesus charged them to repent and to go back and do their first works over. He has evidently been calling His church back to first-works foundational simplicity for a long time.

When the first three verses in this second chapter of Revelation are read, we find that seemingly the Ephesian church did—and was still doing—everything right. They had labored. They had worked. They could not bear those who were evil. They had found out those who were liars. They had persevered. They had been patient. They had labored for His name's sake and not become weary.

However, leaving their first love seemed to have been inexorably tied to their first work. It was serious enough that they were in danger of having their candlestick removed if they did not quickly repent and go back to do their first works again.

Whatever the case, the seven verses immediately following Paul's admonishment in Ephesians 6:10–11 to put on the armor of God stand as tenets today to the importance of being prepared before engaging in fiery battles with the enemy.

While we have grasped the importance of our armor to some degree in the past, what has not remained apparent—and is possibly hidden—is the fact that it is *God's* armor that keeps us centered and focused on Him in the midst of His fire, as well as in the enemy's fire. Keeping our eyes on Him in the midst of both fires is essential for victory.

The following verse-by-verse synopsis on these seven verses from the Book of Ephesians—starting with Ephesians 6:12—will prayerfully birth a renewed understanding and emphasis upon the uncompromising necessity for God's armor in our lives each hour of every day. It is more essential now than ever if we are to continue successfully to fight the good fight of faith unto absolute victory.

THE ARMOR'S TWO FUNCTIONS

> For we do not wrestle against flesh and blood, but against principalities, against powers, against the rulers of the darkness of this age, against spiritual hosts of wickedness in the heavenly places.
> —EPHESIANS 6:12

In this conflict we can no longer afford the fleshly luxury of waging any portion of it in the natural. Nor can we fight the majority of it in the Spirit and periodically lapse back into the flesh. The most ingenious Christian will fall into abject failure and spiritual defeat in these last days if he continues to fight his fiery warfare in the flesh.

It took Calvary to defeat the most brilliant angelic being that God ever created. The devil, together with our own corrupted flesh, the carnal mind and sin nature, required nothing less than the ultimate sacrifice before the armor could be fashioned and purchased. Victory will never be purchased by any other means. All He asks of us in return is that we follow His example by crucifying our flesh through faith in Him.

> Then He said to them all, "If anyone desires to come after Me, let him deny himself, and take up his cross daily, and follow Me."
> —LUKE 9:23

We must master the ability to fight in the spirit realm while remaining continually clothed in God's fiery armor. His fiery armor will simultaneously do two things: 1) It will allow God's fiery glory to consume our carnal flesh as the armor conflicts with every yet-living unholy substance with which it comes into contact; 2) It will protect us as we continue to destroy the manifold works of the devil.

How is He able to do that? Only by our allowing Him to

do it! He will never take our free will away from us. We must remember that the glory of our God is the same yesterday, today and forever—an all-consuming fire. He loves us enough to bring forth glory in our lives by consuming every impeding piece of flesh with which the armor comes into contact as it (the flesh) wars against the spirit and the promise of total victory. Only a multifaceted God can do that. He is doing it while His fiery armor is positioned to destroy the works of the evil one.

Remember, those two simultaneous scenarios are everlastingly taking place in the spirit realm. There is an urgency in the Holy Spirit to be able to discern the relevance in our lives.

Our Lord's plan for our lives has always been conceived in love for our highest good. His purpose is to bring us forth from His refining fires as pure vessels to shine forth God's glory while accomplishing His perfect will. At the same time, we know that the enemy's fiery attacks will always be aimed at our destruction.

Both of these fires remain fully operational at all times, and when we lose sight of that we stand in danger of losing our wrestling match with the enemy, whether that enemy is our flesh or Satan.

Until we discern that *both* fiery positions exist *at all times*, we will not be able to understand or discern God's fiery presence and its purpose in our lives. We need to trust that glorious fire as God's highest love for each of us.

THREE GROUND RULES FOR VICTORY

> Therefore take up the whole armor of God, that you may be able to withstand in the evil day, and having done all, to stand.
> —EPHESIANS 6:13

From the beginning, the Lord has made two things very

clear in His Word. First, we will be unable to stand if we do not fight equipped with His armament provision for our protection. His fiery armor will destroy all the hindering flesh as well as enemy spirits with which it comes into contact. Second, we will not be able to stand without the entire, full and complete armor—not even one piece missing.

Although the Word describes putting on His armor one piece at a time, *nowhere* in the Word does it say to *take it off.* We are to check and examine it daily or as many times as is deemed necessary to assure that it is intact and undamaged—but we are *never to take it off.* So at this point, we already have three essential ground rules for victory established in the first two verses:

- It is going to take the *full armor,* with *nothing left off.*
- It is going to take *all* we know to do, allowing only the Spirit to lead and operate.
- Having so done, we *cannot* back down; we are to *stand!*

> Stand therefore, having your loins girt about with truth, and having on the breastplate of righteousness.
> —EPHESIANS 6:14, KJV

In the Bible, repeated usages of a specific word have always been used when God chooses to penetrate our spiritual eyes and ears: "Simon, Simon" and "Saul, Saul" are but examples of calling His people to highest awareness (Luke 22:31; Acts 9:4). Each time a word or phrase is repeated two or more times in the same verse or context, it is the Lord's spiritual amplification, multiplying the magnitude of that word's importance.

The Lord calls us to attention in Ephesians, saying, "*Stand.* (Its triple enunciation is intended as a spiritual red flag in the fighting of your warfare.) Avail yourself always of My victorious promises, as great diligence will be required in guarding every action in your heart and spirit."

Knowing the significance of His word *stand* is the key: "Having done all, to stand." The Lord says it is imperative that *we keep on standing* no matter how difficult or impossible it may appear in the natural. That triple use of the word *stand* is a clarion call that we are not to yield any territory or ground for which we have fought back the enemy. Period.

THE BELT OF TRUTH

The Greek word for *loins* in verse 14 is the word *osphus*, which means "externally, the area around the hips that are protecting internally the procreative power of the loins." The spiritual implication of the words "procreative power" is not only made clear by its natural meaning, but it is extraordinary in its implication.

This is the very first piece of armor we are told to put on. The *truth* of God must first be acknowledged and activated in us by and through the Holy Spirit. Only God's truth is able to cover and protect *all* of our procreative spiritual components and keep them triumphantly ruling over the deceptive domain of the flesh and the evil one's spirit world. The Lord charges us to apply it first because it is His truth alone that must cover, guard and protect all of our prolific creative powers in the spirit realm.

God's belt or girdle of truth is the *only* assurance and protection we have that what is being produced and created by us in the spirit realm is pure and in accordance with the plumb line of His Word and the sovereign will of a holy God. This essential and vital protective girdle of truth is inherently woven from three basic scriptural components of God:

- *Jesus*—He said, "I am the way, the truth, and the life" (John 14:6).

- *The Word*—Jesus prayed, "Sanctify them by Your truth. Your word is truth" (John 17:17).

- *The Holy Spirit*—Jesus has given us the Holy Spirit, the Spirit of truth (John 14:16–17; 15:26, 16:13).

There are no more powerful weapons available to us than these three all-controlling holy components that make up God's belt of truth.

THE BREASTPLATE OF RIGHTEOUSNESS

The second piece of armor in Ephesians 6:14 is *the breastplate of righteousness.* In His wisdom, God places the breastplate second rather than first.

There is no way we can put on His breastplate of righteousness until we first have His truth around our spiritually creative loins protecting our procreative powers. God's creative power of truth alone must be operating through all our thoughts, spoken words, emotions and actions.

Why are these two pieces important enough for God to record them first? In addition to what has already been defined, it is because without grasping the truth, we have no righteousness of our own in the battle against the enemy of our souls.

Our righteousness has been imputed to us by grace through faith with our belief in Jesus Christ and His completed work on the cross. "For He made Him who knew no sin to be sin for us, that we might become the righteousness of God in Him" (2 Cor. 5:21).

Without the belt of truth to proclaim His truth—who

paid the ultimate price to acquire this breastplate of righteousness, how He obtained it and why—the breastplate of righteousness would not be able to protect the most vulnerable part of our spiritual body from deception: *our hearts*.

> The heart is deceitful above all things, and desperately wicked; who can know it?
> —JEREMIAH 17:9

> Every way of a man is right in his own eyes, but the LORD weighs the hearts.
> —PROVERBS 21:2

Only God's righteous breastplate is capable of knowing and covering this heart of ours purely enough and faithfully enough to protect it from the incessant barrage of Satan's fiery missiles and from lethal flesh, which emit their toxins and poisons of persecutions, offenses, temptations and vanities in all deceitfulness and treachery.

> For out of the abundance of the heart the mouth speaks.
> —MATTHEW 12:34

> Keep your heart with all diligence, for out of it spring the issues of life.
> —PROVERBS 4:23

> With the merciful You will show Yourself merciful; with a blameless man You will show Yourself blameless; with the pure You will show Yourself pure; and with the devious You will show Yourself shrewd. For You will save the humble people, but will bring down haughty looks.
> —PSALM 18:25–27

We have never been capable of knowing our hearts. The Lord alone discerns the heart by His truth and righteousness. The belt of truth and breastplate of righteousness are our infallible protection against the heart's perpetual susceptibility to all the deceptive wiles of carnal flesh and the devil. These two pieces of armor must never be out of place or missing.

Foot Armor of Peace

And having shod your feet with the preparation of the gospel of peace.

—Ephesians 6:15

It is interesting that the third piece of armor is for our feet. Why would God "jump" from the upper portion of the body, for which the first two pieces of our armor are intended, to the very bottom and begin dealing with the feet?

To be able to grasp His reasons more fully, we may need to familiarize ourselves again with an important fact from the contextual reading of God's Word.

Throughout Scripture there are certain spiritual factors that God chooses to emphasize by incorporating them *sequentially as priorities.* Such priorities are sequential because of their need to be considered and understood in God's order of being first, second and so on. Almost without exception the one to be given the greatest urgency and emphasis is written first. They are written in a particular order for a God-breathed reason.

We miss the Lord so often, either by not realizing this fact about God's sequential order or by not endeavoring to understand *why* He has ordered it that way. Nowhere is that more evident than in the understanding of God's directive given to Paul concerning the sequential order of the armor.

To understand why Scripture records the foot armor of peace as the next piece of armor, we must understand that God has always considered our being a witness a prime order of kingdom business—we are to proclaim the kingdom with every step we take.

Could it be that the Lord considers we are not equipped for that vital kingdom assignment until after some "first-things-first" are in order in our own lives? If we take these verses in God's sequential order, He seems to be saying clearly that we are not equipped until two things have happened. First, we must have our powerful procreative forces of the Spirit guarded by His truth. Second, we are not prepared until we have His righteousness protecting our hearts.

Then, and only then, will we be spiritually equipped and ready to walk in His footsteps, sharing the Good News with His little ones in true effectiveness and righteous integrity.

> Arise, walk in the land through its length and its width, for I give it to you.
>
> —GENESIS 13:17

> Every place that the sole of your foot will tread upon I have given you, as I said to Moses.
>
> —JOSHUA 1:3

> Every place on which the sole of your foot treads shall be yours.
>
> —DEUTERONOMY 11:24

We ourselves, however, are the ones who must carry out the preparation by our prayerful study and assimilation of the Word through the Holy Spirit. There is no other way. Scripture tells us we must *prepare* to be His witnesses in order to declare the Good News of His gospel of peace.

This is the Lord's loving prerequisite for dispensing His Word and the peace found in His Word. We have received the charge to show ourselves approved as unashamed workers for Jesus Christ, competent to rightfully divide the word of truth, just as Paul exhorted in 2 Timothy 2:15.

Only by studying to know the Word are we able to absorb and assimilate this glorious gospel all the way through us right down to our spiritual toes and feet. That is the way to have our feet shod and covered with His limitless love of reconciliation and peace found in the gospel. The encasing of our feet with His Word and peace is our protection so that every step we take is sure and guarded from being diverted or detoured.

We know the shoes God supplied to the Israelites miraculously never wore out during their forty years of wilderness journeyings. But have we stopped to think that He has made an even more miraculous provision for our Promised Land journey with our gospel footwear? These gospel shoes of peace will *never* wear out. They were made everlastingly indestructible. They will victoriously outlast all the perils and hazards of our journey to heaven's eternity.

The more that we study His Word, clothed in God's armor of truth and righteousness, the better fitting will be our indestructible gospel shoes of peace. What a God we serve!

It is no longer possible in the ever-encroaching darkness of this age to fight the enemy's battles without being in the center of God's peace and shod with the gospel of peace.

> And the God of *peace* will crush Satan *under your feet* shortly.
> —ROMANS 16:20, EMPHASIS ADDED

It is only from the center of His peace that we are prepared to fight. We first need to master the understanding of this gospel of peace for ourselves in battle before attempting to impart that peace to anyone else. Then we can become truly effective in bringing this gospel of peace to a lost and dying world with every step we take.

THE SHIELD OF FAITH

> Above all, taking the shield of faith with which you will be able to quench all the fiery darts of the wicked one.
>
> —EPHESIANS 6:16

Above all! This is said as God's imperative. The word *all* in the Word always literally means "without exception." This is strong wordage. We already know we've been commanded to put on the full armor, so He is *not* saying, "If you happen to leave off a few pieces, it's okay; just try to make sure you have on the most important pieces, like the shield of faith." NO!

What He *is* saying is:

> But without faith it is impossible to please Him.
>
> —HEBREWS 11:6

What He *is* saying is:

> Whatsoever is not of faith is sin.
>
> —ROMANS 14:23, KJV

What He *is* saying is:

> And this is the victory that has overcome the world— our faith.
>
> —1 JOHN 5:4

Faith is the only piece of God's armor that not only

makes up the shield, but when it is combined with love, it also becomes an integral component of the breastplate of righteousness!

> But let us who are of the day be sober, putting on the breastplate of faith and love.
> —1 THESSALONIANS 5:8

This shield of faith is the most transcendent of all God's weapons. Only love is greater. "Now abide faith, hope, love, these three; but the greatest of these is love" (1 Cor. 13:13). And love never fails because it is the very essence of God, forged in His consuming fire.

We are only underscoring what God has already underscored. He has forged His shield of faith so strongly that it will quench not most of the darts, but *all* of the fiery darts of the enemy. There is that *all* again—God's imperative.

These imperatives are but one way of declaring that our faith shield will not allow even one enemy missile to carry out its intended destructive plan. As long as we keep our faith in God and His protective shield, none of Satan's fiery missiles will be left unquenched. That is not only endlessly impressive, it is victoriously powerful.

THE HELMET OF SALVATION

> And take the helmet of salvation...
> —EPHESIANS 6:17

There is no more critical or indispensable piece of equipment than the helmet of our salvation for the protection and guarding of our mind and thoughts from the enemy. Although this is the fifth piece of armor we are told about in Ephesians 6, yet our salvation is the very first thing made known and extended to us by our confession and His grace.

So why did the Lord wait so long to bring this fifth piece to our attention in His sequential checklist of the armor?

To more thoroughly understand why, let's look at the four pieces He has already brought to our awareness and the order in which He brought them:

1. The belt of *truth*, protecting our spiritual reproductive loins
2. The breastplate of *righteousness*
3. The preparation of the gospel of *peace*, shod on our feet
4. The shield of *faith*

When we begin to reflect on the truth of our righteousness and peace in God, it produces the faith that is the joy of our salvation in the kingdom of God. We have had salvation from the moment we said *yes* to Jesus Christ. But the sixth chapter of Ephesians teaches us that it is also going to take that same helmet to wage successful spiritual warfare against the fiery assault of Satan's indictments, charges and accusations—and from our own carnal flesh—in order to guard and protect our mind and thoughts.

> For to be carnally minded is death, but to be spiritually minded is life and peace.
>
> —ROMANS 8:6

> And do not be conformed to this world, but be transformed by the renewing of your mind, that you may prove what is that good and acceptable and perfect will of God.
>
> —ROMANS 12:2

> And be renewed in the spirit of your mind.
>
> —EPHESIANS 4:23

But we have the mind of Christ.

—1 CORINTHIANS 2:16

Casting down arguments [imaginations] and every high thing that exalts itself against the knowledge of God, bringing every thought into captivity to the obedience of Christ.

—2 CORINTHIANS 10:5

No wonder it took the fiery passion and work of Jesus Christ to forge the helmet for our mind. The thoughts and reasonings of the carnal mind must be transformed and then constantly protected by the Christ mind in order to defeat all the mind games of the devil—not to mention our own carnal thoughts and desires that will continue to be birthed daily if we do not crucify them daily. The helmet of salvation keeps the Christ mind anchored in our thoughts and life as we confront the enemies of our soul.

Nothing takes the constant assault and bombardment that our minds and thoughts take from the three enemies we face each day: our flesh, the world and the devil. None of these three will ever let up until we see Him face to face. The mind, more than anything or anyone else, is indeed the ultimate battlefield of the soul.

With these first five pieces of armor, we have been equipped with five crucial spiritual ornaments:

- Truth
- Righteousness
- Peace
- Faith
- The mind of Christ

THE SWORD OF THE SPIRIT

There is yet another weapon in God's arsenal described in Ephesians 6:17:

...and the sword of the Spirit, which is the word of God.

Now, and only now, are we amply prepared and qualified to not only apply the Word, but—having rightfully divided it in preparation—we are now ready to fight with it, using our proficiency in the Word as our sword. The amount of time we have taken engrafting and forging God's Word in our life will determine how long, sharp and deadly our sword of the Spirit will be.

Many of us are fighting profoundly dangerous enemies with a dwarfed, dull, miniature sword. And we wonder why we are not cutting off the enemies' heads. The one sure remedy? We must take the time to read, learn and equip ourselves, forging and wielding a mightier weapon—God's all-powerful sword of the Spirit. Grasp it firmly in our minds, hearts and spirits. Above all else, steadfastly wield it by the words of our mouths and by our actions. Such a sword is indeed of God's Spirit and carries His guarantee of total victory.

> For the word of God is living and powerful, and sharper than any two-edged sword, piercing even to the division of soul and spirit, and of joints and marrow, and is a discerner of the thoughts and intents of the heart.
> —HEBREWS 4:12

There is no more powerful and dangerous weapon in God's arsenal than the Word of God. Both the written (*logos*) and the spoken (*rhema*) Word of God can be used to either wound or heal.

Logos

Logos is the Greek word for *word*, which means "the complete, whole Word of God, the entire discourse, and all the communication that comprises it."

An example of the Greek word *logos* from the New Testament is found in Hebrews 4:12, referring to the ways in which God's sword effects and executes. Substituting the Greek word *logos* for *word* it reads: "For the *logos* of God is living and powerful. . . . " The whole and complete Word of God, all of His Word in its totality, is living and powerful. Other scriptures that are clear examples can be found in 1 John 1:1; 1 Peter 1:23 and John 1:1.

Rhema

Rhema is the Greek word for *God's word* when it means "a specific thought, a particular thought lifted up out of the whole Word of God." Quite often it is, or has been, a spoken word or thought.

A wonderful scriptural example of the Greek word *rhema* can be found in the tenth chapter of Romans. By substituting *rhema* for *word* in Romans 10:8, we read: "The *rhema* is near you, in your mouth and in your heart." Other instances using the Greek word *rhema* are found in Acts 11:16; Matthew 26:75 and Luke 5:5.

GOD'S CHARGE TO HIS ARMORED SOLDIERS

While studying Ephesians 6, most of us stop with verse 17, which depicts God's last piece of armor. But to do so is to totally miss His reason for charging us to be equipped with the full armor in the first place. It is a charge He would not disclose until all of the armor was complete and thoroughly in place.

Why? Because what He tells us and requires of us next will continuously demand the fullest protection of that armor. It is not until we have all our armor in place, and have understood how essential each piece is, that God considers us protected, equipped and ready for Him to reveal His planned strategy. He knows where and by what method our battles will be enjoined, and He is now ready to give us insight into how the military objective will be fought and won.

This—the strategy on how all warfare battles are to be fought and won—is to be His final directive. He is not switching to a new subject in verse 18. It is an ongoing sentence in thought and punctuation from the preceding seventeenth verse. The climax of this section, it reveals God's primary strategy and purpose for which He gave us the armor:

> Praying always with all prayer and supplication in the Spirit, being watchful to this end with all perseverance and supplication for all the saints.
> —EPHESIANS 6:18

Two major truths must abide in our spirits to fully understand the infinite wisdom of God's ultimate purpose for His armor. First, He has unreservedly prepared us to victoriously win all the fiery battles of the enemy's counterfeit fires that continually rage in every area of our lives. Second—and of equal importance to spiritually assimilate—God's foremost intent in fashioning such power and authority in His armor is to protect His people, who are praying "always!"

In recent years His church has increasingly awakened to the urgency for prayer and intercession, which allows only the Holy Spirit to lead each spiritual conflict. But too few have yet awakened to the equally important reality that prayers are victorious only because of His ultimate provision to empower, guard and protect His church. The invincible and flawless armor purchased at the price of His fiery passion on the cross is our source of protection.

That work of God's ultimate sacrifice on the cross commands a steadfastness in checking and maintaining the armor He died to procure for us. There are no battles in which that protection is more essential than prayer battles and encounters.

It is highly doubtful whether any victory ultimately can be gained without first winning it in the spirit realm through prayer with the fiery armor of God.

Such is the importance of examining and inspecting our armor consistently. That is not possible, however, unless we allow the Holy Spirit to search our lives daily, examining every piece of God's armor for cracks, chinks and missing pieces in the light of His love, from which each piece was equally created. Then, and only then, are we ready for victorious prayer and warfare.

Now we understand more of why it becomes necessary, expedient and very practical to check each piece of our armor daily. We know God's complete armor is His prerequisite for conducting warfare and prayer and intercession. However, when we make that close inspection, it is altogether possible—if not probable—that we will find a need to repair several pieces through repentance and forgiveness. Neglecting to do so will cause damage and deterioration to our armament. But thank God, He is always able to repair, restore and renew whatever damage has incurred if we will just take the remains to Him, confessing where and why the enemy was able to penetrate.

Remember, He is the blacksmith and the goldsmith who blows the coals of those fires, making sure no weapon formed against us will prosper. He can fashion an ever-stronger protection out of our armor through the fiery battles. Not *in spite* of the increased heat from those battles, but actually *because* of them. Thus we find another godly paradox: the hotter the fire, the stronger the spiritual metal being forged from it.

One more correlation begs to be made between God's victorious glory fire, our armor and our prayer and intercession. It again involves the tabernacle plan.

We know that God's pattern and type in that plan was

divided into three main progressions: 1) the outer court; 2) the inner court, which was also called the holy place; and 3) the holy of holies, sometimes called "the most holy place," where the ark of the covenant and the very holy presence of God dwelt.

Two absolutes were required by God before His priests could enter into His presence in the holy of holies. Failure to comply with either of God's two commands was upon penalty of death.

First, the high priest could enter only if he carried the blood from an animal without blemish from off the altar of sacrifice. Jesus Christ paid the ultimate price for that atonement, and His blood now forever flows from Calvary. Second, upon penalty of death, the priests were commanded to take fire from off the golden altar of incense, placing it in the golden censer. That censer, filled with the fiery coals from off the altar of incense, was to burn *perpetually*—the fire never going out—always rising and filling the temple.

Why was it so important to God that the fire from that golden altar of incense burn perpetually?

That was a type of God's glory fire, yet to be fully revealed. The incense from that fire had been sovereignly foreordained as a shadow and type that was being offered in His heavenly throne room. At the same time He would show His church, as His New Covenant priests, that the *substance* from which the pattern had been made had been set in place from the beginning foundations of the world. The Book of Revelation illuminates and unmistakably explains from what the pattern and type had been taken:

> Now when He had taken the scroll, the four living creatures and the twenty-four elders fell down before the Lamb, each having a harp, and golden bowls full of incense, which are the prayers of the saints.
> —REVELATION 5:8

56

Then another angel, having a golden censer, came and stood at the altar. He was given much incense, that he should offer it with the prayers of all the saints upon the golden altar which was before the throne. And the smoke of the incense, with the prayers of the saints, ascended before God from the angel's hand.

—REVELATION 8:3–4

The prayers of the saints have been released upon the fires of the golden altar, freeing them to ascend into the very presence of God. They are continually being released and made manifest. Such is the glory fire out of which our prayers and lives find entry before Him as His own sweet-smelling incense.

For thus says the LORD of hosts: "Once more (it is a little while) I will shake heaven and earth, the sea and dry land; and I will shake all nations, and they shall come to the Desire of All Nations, and I will fill this temple [house] with glory," says the LORD of hosts.

—HAGGAI 2:6–7

4

The Great Shaking

In the very midst of God's glory fire a great shaking is taking place. Haggai prophesied five hundred years before Christ of this violent shaking that would bring forth the glory of the Lord and His body throughout the nations of the world.

Over half a millennium later, the Lord would proclaim it again in Paul's writings to the Hebrew church. This was God's double enunciation to indelibly imprint this prophecy on His people. And so for the second time it would reverberate down through the centuries proclaiming, preparing and warning of the great shaking.

> Surely the Lord GOD does nothing, unless He reveals His secret to His servants the prophets. . . . The Lord GOD has spoken! Who can but prophesy?
> —AMOS 3:7–8

There is little doubt that this great shaking is taking

place now as we face the twilight hours of this dispensation. Today even nonbelievers are turning to biblical conjecturing in their search for answers, as they are beginning to realize there is something bigger out there than just "Mother Nature."

Increased apprehensions, anxieties and fears are being felt in every area of life around this world. The Lord is seeing to it that all people everywhere—the unbeliever as well as the believer—give testimony and confirmation to the unprecedented greatness of these shakings.

In the natural realm there have been earthquakes, floods, pestilence, famines, violence and innumerable other devastating catastrophes that have increased at an exponentially rapid rate all over this earth realm. Jesus foretold in the twenty-fourth chapter of Matthew that these things would come to pass as signs of the great shaking in the End Times.

However, this same great shaking is also taking place in the spirit realm. (For every spiritual operation there will be a natural manifestation!) In God's Word, we are explicitly told that all the spiritual elements will be just as violently shaken as the natural ones.

Who has not felt the truth and reality of that with all of our own spiritual earthquakes, floods, pestilences, famines, tempests and spiritual violence? The throbbing answer is *no one.*

At this point it is pivotal that we establish who or what is doing the shaking. Haggai 2:6 leaves absolutely no room for doubt as to *who* is doing the shaking. It is the Lord God of Abraham, Isaac and Jacob. Even when we understand this dominant truth, many of us will still wrestle with why a loving God not only *allows* such violent shakings, but would be *the initiator* of them. And not only the initiator of them, but the *promisor* of them.

We are scripturally compelled to find the Lord's loving reasons for His great shaking. As always, truth is able to be revealed through the inerrancy of Scripture:

Sanctify them by Your truth. Your word is truth.
—JOHN 17:17

See that you do not refuse Him who speaks. For if they did not escape who refused Him who spoke on earth, much more shall we not escape if we turn away from Him who speaks from heaven, whose voice then shook the earth; but now He has promised, saying, "Yet once more I shake not only the earth, but also heaven."
—HEBREWS 12:25–26

Not only was this shaking a prophecy that would be fulfilled—it was also one of His never-failing promises. The immediate question that presents itself is, "But God, why?" He answers that in the next three verses:

"Yet once more," indicates the removal of those things that are being shaken, as of things that are made, that the things which cannot be shaken may remain. Therefore, since we are receiving a kingdom which cannot be shaken, let us have grace, by which we may serve God acceptably with reverence and godly fear. For our God is a consuming fire.
—HEBREWS 12:27–29

God's loving, fiery objective just became very clear. He intends to shake everything from our lives that is not of Him—all those ingredients we keep attempting to use in the building of our earthly house, His temple, that are made from substances other than the Rock and His unshakeable things of the kingdom. The consuming fire of God is shaking all things, and He always begins with His church.

For the time has come for judgment to begin at the house of God; and if it begins with us first, what will be the end of those who do not obey the gospel of God?

—1 PETER 4:17

Our God shall come, and shall not keep silent; a fire shall devour before Him, and it shall be very tempestuous all around Him. He shall call to the heavens from above, and to the earth, that He may judge His people. "Gather My saints together to Me, those who have made a covenant with Me by sacrifice."

—PSALM 50:3–5

In a parable, Jesus warned us what the results would be if we allowed our house to be built—or to stay built—on the unstable sands of our own will, our own ways and our own desires. Remember, He made it very clear that the stormy shakings would come to both houses, regardless of where and how the houses were built.

Therefore whoever hears these sayings of Mine, and does them, I will liken him to a wise man who built his house on a rock: and the rain descended, the floods came, and the winds blew and beat on that house; and it did not fall, for it was founded [built] on the rock. But everyone who hears these sayings of Mine, and does not do them, will be like a foolish man who built his house on the sand: and the rains descended, the floods came, and the winds blew and beat on that house; and it fell. And great was its fall.

—MATTHEW 7:24–27

So how does a loving God who is a consuming fire survey the Jesus-quality of what we have been building in our lives so that we can see (He already knows) what needs to be repaired, replaced, restored or rebuilt?

What if the beginning firm foundation has become weakened or defective due to some shifting spiritual trespass sands of which we have not repented? What if sands of pride, rebellion or deception have been mixed into that original foundation? How are we to know the truth as our Lord knows it? And of prime importance, how are we going to know if we are fighting the enemy with half our armor missing?

What if one or more pieces of the armor have been damaged due to prideful assumptions, neglect or disregard of prayer? He alone knows the state of our lives and heart. Have we yielded and allowed the Holy Spirit to search and bring God's sword of truth down to the very marrow of our spiritual bones?

The Architect and Chief Engineer of our souls loves us too much not to let us know if we are following the configuration in bringing forth His perfect design, plan and purpose. Engineering stress tests before, during and after are being performed by the Master Engineer who created us in our mother's womb with exacting specifications for His heavenly design.

He is performing the stress tests so that we will discover what areas of our lives need to be renovated and reinforced. He already knows. Wherever and whenever we confront the great shaking of excessive pressures, circumstances, crisis and burdens that expose some frailty, know that it is exposed for only one purpose by God—to be victoriously fortified. The magnitude of our quakes are causing all the previous unexposed areas by which the enemy could gain, or has gained, access to be uncovered.

Each of our finished tabernacles will wear a designer label: "Made Exclusively for the Bride of Christ." "An Original." We are getting the final fittings for our wedding gown! They are not yet a perfect fit because of the spots and wrinkles still on them and in them. But He is in the process of removing the spots and ironing out the wrinkles. We are being escorted by our Bridegroom through our final preparations.

Often we cannot see in order to rectify that which the enemy has hidden in our lives. That is why the Lord is seeing to it that those things that were once hidden in darkness are now being brought into His marvelous light. He wants us to come to Him, relinquishing everything so completely that each life is impervious to future shakings by God—and every attack of the enemy.

This applies especially to the massive damage that can be caused when any portion of our spiritual frame has been left exposed because some piece of the protective armor has been forgotten or left out in the elements of the world to rust and corrode. Our armor must be freshly oiled with the anointing oil of the Holy Spirit each day.

The standard against which our Architect and Chief Engineer is conducting these tests is the character of God's Son with the fruit of the Holy Spirit. We, as the vessels of the Lord, should continuously be filled with the fresh oil of the Holy Spirit, which contains the fruit of the Spirit and character of Jesus Christ as the new wine from the true Vine (Gal. 5:22–23).

As His body, we have freely received this precious gift from the Vinedresser and the Vine. But along with this free gift we have also been given the charge to freely pour out the oil and the wine. This fruit and wine, together with the priceless oil of the Holy Spirit, have been given to bring a healing balm to a lost and dying world.

> I am the true vine, and My Father is the vinedresser. Every branch in Me that does not bear fruit He takes away; and every branch that bears fruit He prunes, that it may bear more fruit.
>
> —John 15:1–2

The Vine—Jesus—went to the cross for us in order to pay the price for those plantings—His branches—to produce the new wine and the fruit of the Spirit. The Lord is continually tending, pruning and preparing His branches to bear the unspotted, unblemished fruit from His vine. He intends for His branches to produce much fruit, which will not only remain, but will taste as pure, sweet and fulfilling as the perfect first fruit from which it came (John 15:16).

But this presents a problem of no small proportion. The problem is perhaps best explained by continuing the vineyard analogy as to the wine itself and how it is created. The crushing of the grapes is an uncompromising and necessary step in the producing of wine.

After all of the pulp and waste—all of our flesh—is extracted, only the very *heart* of the fruit will remain. But if any sediments, dregs and impurities are allowed to remain, they will make their way to the very bottom of the wine vessel, where the dregs appear to be almost invisible to the natural eye.

The wine may be poured out at first with very little detection of its having been compromised by not going through the entire exacting and meticulous process of being crushed, filtered and poured back and forth, back and forth, back and forth, continually through ever finer filters. If that compromise is allowed to continue through to the final stages of the wine process, all of its contaminants will neither be detected nor removed.

But just give the contents of that compromising vessel of wine a sudden *jarring or shaking*. All of its settled and hidden acrid properties are suddenly released throughout the wine, which had previously appeared to be pure, unclouded and unblemished. Now it is expelling a harsh, bitter flavor with each drop that is poured and tasted.

Thank You, Lord, not only for being the vine that is our purifying filtering system for Your wine, but also, by Your Holy Spirit, for being our new wineskins as well.

Nor do they put new wine into old wineskins, or else the wineskins break, the wine is spilled, and the

> wineskins are ruined. But they put new wine into new
> wineskins, and both are preserved.
>
> —MATTHEW 9:17

He produces our new wineskins in the Spirit as the Israelites created them in the natural—by thoroughly rubbing them with new oil (the new anointing oil of the Holy Spirit) over and over and over again.

Everything that can be shaken is indeed being shaken. God's ways are so much higher than our ways. His compassionate purpose is to shake off everything in our lives that is not an integral part of our Lord.

These are the times when we need to remember that God has just as unequivocally promised that everything in our lives that is of Him will remain. It cannot be shaken.

PRAYER

In these last days everything that has not been filtered through prayer will be shaken and will not stand. Everywhere we turn we are hearing more and more about prayer. That is the Lord's Spirit enunciating again and again how essential is the prayer life of His church.

Have you noticed there are less and less circumstances that can be victoriously dealt with without more and more prevailing prayer?

God is shaking prayerless lives down to His kingdom's firm foundation of prayer and intercession. There is no other way to stand on the firm foundation of Jesus Christ, whose very life was made up of constant communication with the Father through prayer. From the throne room in the heavenlies He is still leading us in prayer by His example.

> Therefore He is also able to save to the uttermost those who come to God through Him, since He always lives to make intercession for them.
>
> —HEBREWS 7:25

Our continual prayer charge is both explicit and impossible without the work of the cross and the Holy Spirit.

> Then He spoke a parable to them, that men always ought to pray and not lose heart.
> —LUKE 18:1

> Pray without ceasing.
> —1 THESSALONIANS 5:17

> But constant prayer was offered to God for him by the church.
> —ACTS 12:5

> For this reason we also, since the day we heard it, do not cease to pray for you, and to ask that you may be filled with the knowledge of His will in all wisdom and spiritual understanding.
> —COLOSSIANS 1:9

These Scriptures are not just vague generalizations expressing God's desire for us to pray *sometimes*. If He had just said "always" once it would be a literal command and charge. But He proclaims it *again and again and again*. This is the prayer standard that Jesus lived here on earth as our example and is still living in heaven.

This is the same command laid down for God's priests from the beginning, when He commanded the incense to burn continuously upon the altar and never go out:

> He shall burn incense upon it, a perpetual incense before the LORD throughout your generations.
> —EXODUS 30:8

And in the last book of the Bible, God reveals what that perpetual incense is:

> . . . and golden bowls full of incense, which are the
> prayers of the saints.
> —REVELATION 5:8

His church is going to be a praying church. His bride will purely reflect His prayer life. His very character, embodied by the nine fruits of the Spirit, will be held together and sanctified by prayer. If we have something left to do for God and feel called by Him to do it, if we do not achieve it from a foundation of prayer, it will not stand.

HUMILITY

The Lord is shaking down the evil fruit of pride in His body whenever and wherever He finds it—both natural pride and spiritual pride. He is also bringing down the reverse of that pride from the other end of the spectrum—that is, the equally evil fruit of false humility, which is an elusive pride that masquerades as humbleness, and an inverted pride, which often manifests itself as the enemy's condemnation and shame rather than God's conviction.

> When swelling and pride come, then emptiness and
> shame come also.
> —PROVERBS 11:2, AMP

Condemnation and *conviction* are literally of two different worlds. *Condemnation* is from the fires of hell and is fueled by the hatred of Satan for God's children. *Conviction*, on the other hand, is from the consuming fire of God and is fueled by His everlasting love for us.

The fires of condemnation from the devil will make us feel that there is no hope, no love, no mercy—in short, no atoning blood or work of the cross—and it is completely loveless: "That is the third time this week you've done that. Do you really think you're going to be able to change? God's not going to put up with this forever, you know.

Don't you know He's sick of your saying that you're trying?"

There's not an ounce of love or truth in those words, only mocking hate and destruction, which tells us who is doing the talking. Such satanic fruit produces feelings that we will never be worthy. Who said that? Not Jesus. Our eternal worth has been written in His blood and sealed by His cross. Who are we ever to tell Him—or to let the devil tell us—that we're not worthy in Him?

> There is therefore now no condemnation to those who are in Christ Jesus, who do not walk according to the flesh, but according to the Spirit.
> —ROMANS 8:1

The only time that condemnation becomes a plumb line in God's hand is when we refuse to leave the enemy's world of darkness, choosing to live with darkened, deceived and unrepentant hearts.

> And this is the condemnation, that the light has come into the world, and men loved darkness rather than light, because their deeds were evil.
> —JOHN 3:19

On the other hand, God's conviction has always been directed from His everlasting love. It is His eternal motive and purpose even when He chastens. "My child, do not go any further down that road. Have you not yet seen it is not of Me? There is no love on that path, only the enemy's thorns to destroy. It will cause you more pain, and there is much danger ahead. Stop, and turn around. Come back to Me, and let My blood cleanse the wounds and heal the pain."

> For whom the LORD loves He chastens, and scourges every son whom He receives. If you endure chastening,

> God deals with you as sons; for what son is there
> whom a father does not chasten?
> —HEBREWS 12:6–7

> For they indeed for a few days chastened us as seemed
> best to them, but He for our profit, that we may be
> partakers of His holiness.
> —HEBREWS 12:10

The Lord is preparing His FireBride by assigning her the final exams, given by the Holy Spirit. There is only *one* correct answer to every true-or-false and multiple-choice question given to us, regardless of how difficult, extreme or seemingly impossible the situation is.

The only correct and unequivocal answer to every question from now until we see Him face to face is that our true identity and walk lie exclusively in Jesus Christ at *all times*. That's it. Period. Over and out. No other answers are being accepted.

He is teaching us, by ever narrowing tolerances to any answer that is not God's answer, what the consequences are when we do not walk in the light of our true identity in Him. It is no longer without consequence—no matter how irrelevant or insignificant the occasion might seem to us— to walk according to the darkness of our flesh.

> For from within, out of the heart of men, proceed evil
> thoughts . . . covetousness, wickedness, deceit . . . pride,
> foolishness. All these evil things . . . defile a man.
> —MARK 7:21–23

> For all that is in the world—the lust of the flesh, the
> lust of the eyes, and the pride of life—is not of the
> Father but is of the world.
> —1 JOHN 2:16

As we follow God's pillar of fire through these seasoning

situations, our pride is being shaken and burned out. This is the testing and proving of God's promise through Paul, who says, "[We] can do all things through Christ who strengthens [us]" (Phil. 4:13).

We cannot successfully accomplish anything for God if we do not know who we are in Christ Jesus. We are *overcomers*. But we will not be victorious in these last days if we allow the leaven of pride to remain while attempting to feed on the Bread of Life.

> He who has an ear, let him hear what the Spirit says to the churches. To him who overcomes I will give some of the hidden manna to eat. And I will give him a white stone, and on the stone a new name written which no one knows except him who receives it.
> —REVELATION 2:17

The Greek word for *overcomes* and *overcomer* is *nikao*. It appears twenty-eight times in twenty-four scriptures in five books of the New Testament: Luke, John, Romans, 1 John and Revelation. It means "to subdue (literally or figuratively)—to conquer, overcome, prevail, get the victory."

> But when a stronger than he comes upon him and overcomes him, he takes from him all his armor in which he trusted, and divides his spoils.
> —LUKE 11:22

> And he who overcomes, and keeps My works until the end, to him I will give power over the nations.
> —REVELATION 2:26

> And they overcame him by the blood of the Lamb and by the word of their testimony, and they did not love their lives to the death.
> —REVELATION 12:11

As God continues to pull down false pride and the inverse pride of condemnation, we must remember that without exception He exposes only to reveal more of our true identity in Him. Just as tenaciously He is pulling down all glory-seeking spiritual pride no matter how deceptively "innocent" it may seem: "Did you hear about the miracle that happened when *I prayed?*"

Yes, but how many others prayed who are known only to the Lord? And whose power alone provided the answer?

Our deceptive hearts are being taught the final lessons about all forms of pride straight from God's throne room. All the glory belongs to God, and it is His alone to bestow.

> The LORD will destroy the house of the proud.
> —PROVERBS 15:25

> Therefore humble yourselves under the mighty hand of God, that He may exalt you in due time.
> —1 PETER 5:6

> Jesus said to them, "If you were blind, you would have no sin; but now you say, 'We see.' Therefore your sin remains."
> —JOHN 9:41

As we overcome God's shakings, not only are we being prepared to seek God's flaming light, but we are also being prepared to walk continually in it. We cannot see that light if our eyes are blinded by any form of natural or spiritual pride. No one will be able to walk in His light in these last days without humility. Once again, here is the awesome love of God fashioning His precious vessels of honor.

> A man's pride will bring him low, but the humble in spirit will retain honor.
> —PROVERBS 29:23

> Each of you should know how to possess his own vessel in sanctification and honor.
>
> —1 THESSALONIANS 4:4

From now until we see Him, we are also being called upon to receive and give extraordinary amounts of God's grace. James and Peter counsel us that God's grace is unequaled when it is fashioned from humility, but the price of pride demands God's strongest restraints.

> Yes, all of you be submissive to one another, and be clothed with humility, for "God resists the proud, but gives grace to the humble."
>
> —1 PETER 5:5

> He who overcomes shall be clothed in white garments, and I will not blot out his name from the Book of Life; but I will confess his name before My Father and before His angels.
>
> —REVELATION 3:5

With the Lord preparing our wedding garment, the dark stains of any form of pride will not be allowed to remain— whether we consider those stains insignificantly small or not. Only the purity reflected in us through the example of Christ's humility is considered pure enough and white enough to fashion our bridal garment. "Come," the Lord is saying to us now as never before. Though our sin of pride and vanity be as scarlet, He is asking that we come and reason with Him, repenting and allowing His blood to wash us white as snow (Isa. 1:18).

PURPOSE

God is shaking down every purpose, design and objective for our lives that is not of Jesus Christ. That includes, at its very zenith, all of the plans, strategies and attitudes that we have adopted in His natural world as well as in His spiritual world. The twenty-sixth chapter of Acts contains something very remarkable for these last days:

> But rise and stand on your feet; for I have appeared to you for this purpose, to make you a minister and a witness both of the things which you have seen and of the things which I will yet reveal to you.
>
> —ACTS 26:16

These same twofold purposes are being established in our lives today: to be a minister of the gospel of Jesus Christ and to be a witness of two things—that which has already been revealed and that which is yet to be revealed.

As a witness in the high courts of heaven, just as in courts on earth, the only things admissible from witnesses are what they themselves have experienced, seen and known. What they themselves—with their own eyes, ears and mouth—have said, done, believed, expressed and observed. In these last days our becoming such a witness for Jesus Christ is the only valid purpose that will stand in our lives.

God's purposes are going to be elevated, not only as the zenith of our own lives, but equally sought after in the lives of others. Our communication as His ministers is going to reflect that we are partakers of heavenly places as we recount with joy the things we have seen and heard through the power of the Holy Spirit. And with that same singleness of purpose we will relate the experiences He has yet to reveal to us in the future.

Each of us has been given a purpose that parallels that of Acts 26:16. His perfect design for each one of us, taken from His celestial blueprints, is as unique and distinctive as a thumbprint or snowflake. He has used a never-to-be-duplicated emotional and spiritual DNA. He imparts to us the purposes for which He alone has designed us through

His holy calling on our lives. That calling is wondrously ours alone, imparted to us from the throne room of grace even before we were in our mother's womb.

This is the season when every purpose in our life that is not in line with God's purposes will be shaken down to His unshakeable foundation.

> To everything there is a season, a time for every purpose under heaven.
> —ECCLESIASTES 3:1

> And we know that all things work together for good to those who love God, to those who are the called according to His purpose.
> —ROMANS 8:28

> Because to every purpose there is time and judgment.
> —ECCLESIASTES 8:6, KJV

To borrow an expression often used in Christmas rhymes, "Jesus is the reason for this season." And this season is going to last until He comes. To those who desire some other happening to periodically become the reason, there will be little to look forward to except increasing confusion, frustration, unhappiness and despair. The very foundations of our lives are being shaken by His fiery great shakings, consuming every reason for our being here except those found in the foundation of the kingdom of God, with Jesus Christ as the Chief Cornerstone.

> Therefore do not be ashamed of the testimony of our Lord . . . who has saved us and called us with a holy calling, not according to our works, but according to His own purpose and grace which was given to us in Christ Jesus before time began.
> —2 TIMOTHY 1:8–9

All of the gray areas are disappearing as His pure love, together with His great mercy and grace, constrains us to choose those purposes of a risen Christ so that we may be the joyous overcomers of every conflict.

> Now the purpose of the commandment is love from a pure heart, from a good conscience, and from sincere faith.
>
> —1 TIMOTHY 1:5

Three elements remain as God's purpose for the commandment until He comes:

- Love from a pure heart
- Love from a good conscience
- Love from sincere faith

Yet not one of these three is obtainable if we are allowed to retain our own purposes and priorities rather than undividedly holding on to His.

Can we begin to acknowledge why everything that can be shaken *must be shaken?* His incomparable love is preparing a FireBride that has been birthed in His glory fire. Such fiery love will continue to shake down every endeavor, plan and purpose based upon our own priorities and accomplishments—no matter how "good" or "right" they may have seemed in the past—leaving only those eternal purposes that are explicitly Christ-born and Christ-breathed, issuing forth from us by the Holy Spirit.

> LORD, You have heard the desire of the humble; You will prepare their heart; You will cause Your ear to hear.
>
> —PSALM 10:17

The Lord is replacing all the untempered mortar we

have used in building the walls of our temple. (See Ezekiel 13:10–15; 22:28.) Unfortunately, we have also used this same untempered mortar as the bonding agent in our attempts to unite His body in the church. Through fiery great shakings, He is eliminating the defective fleshly mortar mixture, intermingled with weakened portions of the spirit, and replacing it with God's tempered mortar of Jesus Christ's character and anointing.

The perfect prayer that Jesus prayed in John 17 for His church called for our unity. The Father has never allowed one prayer of His Son's to fall to the ground, and neither will He allow this His ultimate prayer—for which He gave His life—to fail.

> Endeavoring to keep the unity of the Spirit in the *bond* of peace.
> —EPHESIANS 4:3, EMPHASIS ADDED

> Therefore, as the elect of God, holy and beloved, put on tender mercies, kindness, humility, meekness, longsuffering; bearing with one another, and forgiving one another, if anyone has a complaint against another; even as Christ forgave you, so you also must do. But above all these things put on love, which is the *bond* of perfection.
> —COLOSSIANS 3:12–14, EMPHASIS ADDED

Thank You, Lord, for loving us too much to allow anything to remain in our lives that does not have the Holy Spirit's tempered bonding agent. We yield and repent, giving back to You once again our soiled, wrinkled garments. Take out the wrinkles and stains that appeared because of all the untempered mortar of our days, causing us to lose our joy by not allowing the bonding agents of Your character to be tempered into our life.

Perseverance

Patience, steadfastness and perseverance in trials, tribulations, testings and persecutions have always been God's victorious hallmarks of the overcoming Christian. Everything that hinders and prevents those virtues of the Lord from becoming dominant in our lives is now being eliminated. He is showing us a great multiplicity of opportunities that strengthen our perseverance, increase patience and maintain steadfastness.

> But also for this very reason, giving all diligence, add to your faith virtue, to virtue knowledge, to knowledge self-control, to self-control perseverance, to perseverance godliness, to godliness brotherly kindness, and to brotherly kindness love.
>
> —2 Peter 1:5–7

> Therefore, my beloved brethren, be steadfast, immovable, always abounding in the work of the Lord, knowing that your labor is not in vain in the Lord.
>
> —1 Corinthians 15:58

> For we have become partakers of Christ if we hold the beginning of our confidence steadfast to the end.
>
> —Hebrews 3:14

> Resist him [Satan], steadfast in the faith, knowing that the same sufferings are experienced by your brotherhood in the world.
>
> —1 Peter 5:9

Persecution is a word we usually shy away from, avoiding discussions about it. Nevertheless, God has always used the adversary's persecutions as instruments in His sovereign hands to increase the church's power, authority and strength, and to mature His bride in the character, unity and love of Jesus Christ.

In Acts, the second chapter, the church was "with one accord in one place" (Acts 2:1). But when persecution came because of their belief in Jesus as the Messiah, we find them described, just two chapters later and as a direct result of those persecutions, as having become "of one heart and one soul":

> Now the multitude of those who believed were of one heart and one soul; neither did anyone say that any of the things he possessed was his own, but they had all things in common.
>
> —ACTS 4:32

> Yes, and all who desire to live godly in Christ Jesus will suffer persecution.
>
> —2 TIMOTHY 3:12

The enemy thought that through persecution he could destroy the just-born infant church. But God used that same persecution for His own sovereign purposes. As a direct result of the persecutions, the disciples were first dispersed, enabling them to carry the Word with them wherever they went. Thus began the spreading to the world of the gospel that Jesus Christ is Lord.

God's people—and the enemy—were once again being taught that there is *nothing* that the Lord cannot and does not use to bring forth His good and His glory. All He asks is that His people trust Him, believe in His promises and stand against the wiles of the enemy with their eyes *single* on Him.

The Lord has given us the unfailing and eternal promise of beauty for ashes. We may not know how. We may not know when. But we do know that what He does will exceed all that we could have thought or asked (Eph. 3:20).

The church today is living with increased darkness, including countless persecutions all over the world. Most of these persecutions and atrocities are taking place in Third World countries; they may appear to be religious or political in nature, but they are demonically motivated. The people in these countries have lived in gross spiritual darkness for hundreds of centuries.

Increasingly Christians are paying the price and laying down their lives sacrificially in order to spread the light of His gospel over the world's spiritual darkness. They stand as courageous confirmation to the fact that the church is continuing to receive His great character, strength and power through His manifold grace, which multiplies expediently and exponentially in times of persecution.

> And with great power the apostles gave witness to the resurrection of the Lord Jesus. And great grace was upon them all.
>
> —ACTS 4:33

The Lord's imparted character to His church is beginning once again to provide a depth of holy passion. It creates a supernatural atmosphere as well as a sacrificial love, which faithfully and joyfully walks through the valley of the shadow of death.

In the Twenty-third Psalm, written almost ten centuries before the cross of Christ, David prophetically saw death as having lost its sting (1 Cor. 15:55–56). He depicted death as only passing through a valley, as fleeting and illusionary as a mere shadow (Ps. 23:4).

Early Christians confirmed the reality of that truth with their uncompromising, joyous willingness to experience death when they were presented with a choice between eternal life with Jesus Christ or the torture and killing of their natural body (Matt. 10:28). More than any other characteristic, the world witnessed the early church's joyful willingness to reduce death to nothing more than a fleeting dark shadow through which they passed on the way to their real destination—eternal life with their Bridegroom in His marvelous light and love:

> We are confident, I say, and willing rather to be absent from the body, and to be present with the Lord.
> —2 CORINTHIANS 5:8, KJV

That characteristic is being witnessed again in His FireBride. Christians undergoing oppression and persecution in different countries and cultures have become increasingly aware that the only thing worth living for is the one thing worth dying for—their Pearl of great price. They are willingly paying that price with their temporal, natural lives.

It is out of the fires and shakings of such extreme conditions and persecutions that a growing, mighty force of steadfast power and love is coming forth. These persecuted Christians are raising up the high sacrificial standard found in Acts. They intimately know, love and live in the fiery presence of their God. Each of us should consider their lives an advanced reality check for our own sacrificial commitment in times of crisis.

> Do not fear any of those things which you are about to suffer. Indeed, the devil is about to throw some of you into prison, that you may be tested, and you will have tribulation ten days. Be faithful until death, and I will give you the crown of life.
> —REVELATION 2:10

One thing needs to be kept in perspective when laying down one's life unreservedly to God: Christians, being human, are not exempt from being blinded at times by enemy deceptions and craftiness. Such deception can render them unable to discern to whom they are yielding their members—to the devil and his fires, or to the Lord's purification fires.

There are basic safeguards that minimize the enemy's ability to perpetrate confusion between the two. The first is to consistently walk and operate in the Holy Spirit, particularly with His discerning of spirits. Only then can we know who is giving the directions. Second is the need to have our experiences evaluated by those in authority who are spiritually mature. They have walked the road ahead of us and are able to see spiritual land mines.

> Where there is no counsel, the people fall; but in the multitude of counselors there is safety.
> —PROVERBS 11:14

> Without counsel, plans go awry, but in the multitude of counselors they are established.
> —PROVERBS 15:22

Thank You, Lord, for leading us back afresh to the beautiful simplicity of Your gospel. So simple to accept, but so impossible to accomplish without Your love guiding us every step of the way and walking with us in the fiery light of Your presence. Thank You for the atoning blood by which we stand before Your throne of grace, sinless and ready to rededicate our lives as never before.

> When you pass through the waters, I will be with you; and through the rivers, they shall not overflow you. When you walk through the fire, you shall not be burned, nor shall the flame scorch you.
> —ISAIAH 43:2

> ...that the things which cannot be shaken may remain.
> —HEBREWS 12:27

All of the heave offerings of the holy things, which the children of Israel offer to the LORD, I have given to you and your sons and daughters with you as an ordinance forever; it is a covenant of salt forever before the LORD with you and your descendants with you.

—NUMBERS 18:19

5

Fire Seasoned With Salt

One of the things the Lord is revealing by His fire in these last days is a renewed awareness that we are to be the salt of the earth and to understand the cost—and rewards—of what that means. It is the one covenant that most members of His body do not know enough about. In these last days as He calls us back to spiritual basics, there is a need to reclaim and recommit to His Salt Covenant.

The Hebrew word for *heave* in Numbers 18:19 means "a present offered up; especially in sacrifice." The Lord enacted the Salt Covenant as an everlasting covenant between Himself and His people from the very beginning.

You may ask, "But wasn't that covenant just until Jesus came and fulfilled all things?" The answer, from Jesus Himself, is *no.*

> For everyone will be seasoned with fire, and every sacrifice will be seasoned with salt.
> —MARK 9:49

Jesus was the fulfillment of every pattern and type in the tabernacle plan, together with all the offerings—not only as God's perfect sacrifice, but also as His high priest.

However, His transcendent purpose for fulfilling the pattern purely, perfectly and completely was to be the first-born of many brethren, so that they could be conformed into the same image (Rom. 8:29). He fulfilled it so that all who believed in Him would not only know redemption, but also be able to inherit all of the Father's eternal promises as joint heirs with His begotten Son:

> ...and if children, then heirs—heirs of God and joint heirs with Christ, if indeed we suffer with Him, that we may also be glorified together.
>
> —ROMANS 8:17

As joint heirs we have inherited all of God's everlasting covenants, including the Salt Covenant. And, as Jesus announced in no uncertain terms from the Mark 9:49 passage, it is still very much a nonnegotiable part of our daily sacrificial lives.

Since it is an everlasting covenant, what are the spiritual ramifications and conditions that comprise this covenant of salt? What is it, and what does it mean to one's daily life and walk with Him? What aspect of our lives are we to season with it? Every aspect? How are we to keep it?

We gain insight by examining some of the major characteristics of natural salt:

- It purifies.
- It cleanses.
- It preserves.
- It enhances.
- It seasons.
- It penetrates.
- It heals.
- It flavors.

And every offering of your grain offering you shall season with salt; you shall not allow the salt of the

covenant of your God to be lacking from your grain offering. With *all* your offerings you shall offer salt.
—LEVITICUS 2:13, EMPHASIS ADDED

There should be no argument that the grain in the grain offering is representative of the Word of God, the gospel, and of Jesus, who is the Word made flesh, the Bread of Life. We are, as specific individual members of His body, abiding in Him as an indivisible part of that grain offering. We are partakers with Him in providing and giving the same grain offering and the Bread of Life.

For we being many are one bread, and one body: for we are all partakers of that one bread.
—1 CORINTHIANS 10:17, KJV

We partake of the Lord's grain offerings and Bread of Life in order to provide that same grain offering and Bread of Life to others. "Freely you have received, freely give" (Matt. 10:8). That has always been His clarion call for everything He purchased for us on the cross. He gave His life for us so that we, in turn, could give His life to others.

This commandment to give freely to all is precisely the reason we can no longer remain indifferent to the Salt Covenant between us and our Lord. As He restores all things to His church this covenant will once again prevail as the means of seasoning the life given to Him and for others. The keeping of the Salt Covenant is an essential component in the preparation of the daily commitments we offer to Him.

He has already supplied us with His grain for our grain offerings, His salt for our Salt Covenant and His being as our Bread of Life. To whatever degree we relinquish our wills by daily crucifying the flesh to receive these impartations, to that same degree they become ours to offer back up to Him in joyous praise and thanksgiving, and then to offer it all to one another and the world.

> Then the priest shall take from the grain offering a memorial portion, and burn it on the altar. It is an offering made by fire, a sweet aroma to the LORD.
> —LEVITICUS 2:9

> You are the salt of the earth; but if the salt loses its flavor, how shall it be seasoned? It is then good for nothing but to be thrown out and trampled underfoot by men.
> —MATTHEW 5:13

Some characteristics of our spiritual salt, if compromised, could cause that salt to lose its flavor in our lives. We need to take a closer look at each of the characteristics of His spiritual salt. As we do, we will understand the consequences should one of the ingredients be missing or its flavor lost. What does it take to receive and retain all these characteristics in our lives? Absolutely nothing—except less of us and more of Him.

SALT PURIFIES

Nothing is a more important characteristic of spiritual salt than the fact that it purifies.

> Beloved, now we are children of God; and it has not yet been revealed what we shall be, but we know that when He is revealed, we shall be like Him, for we shall see Him as He is. And everyone who has this hope in Him purifies himself, just as He is pure.
> —1 JOHN 3:2–3

> Blessed are the pure in heart, for they shall see God.
> —MATTHEW 5:8

Scripture makes it clear that this purification is something we must effect ourselves. While the Lord has given us all the necessary spiritual means to accomplish purity as salt in our lives, only we can take advantage of these means and put them to work, using them for the purification of our thoughts, emotions, words and actions. How are we to do that? As always, the Word gives us the answer:

> And everyone who has this hope in Him purifies himself, just as He is pure.
>
> —1 JOHN 3:3

> Draw near to God and He will draw near to you. Cleanse your hands, you sinners; and purify your hearts, you double-minded.
>
> —JAMES 4:8

> Since you have purified your souls in obeying the truth through the Spirit in sincere love of the brethren, love one another fervently with a pure heart.
>
> —1 PETER 1:22

Conformity to the truth of the Word, the cleansing blood of the Lamb and the transparency of God's love— these are the three powerful purifying agents of God for our salt. They will provide us with all we need to purify ourselves as His salt every moment of each day.

SALT CLEANSES

Scripture confirms that cleansing is another element of salt that we are to supply for ourselves.

> Wash yourselves, make yourselves clean; put away the evil of your doings from before My eyes. Cease to do evil, learn to do good; seek justice, rebuke the oppressor.
>
> —ISAIAH 1:16–17

> Therefore if anyone cleanses himself . . . he will be a
> vessel for honor, sanctified and useful for the Master,
> prepared for every good work.
>
> —2 TIMOTHY 2:21

After examining scriptures that refer to the cleansing property of spiritual salt, it appears that cleansing requires more consistent reading, studying and hearing of the Word for ourselves than any of the other properties of salt.

> . . . just as Christ also loved the church and gave
> Himself for her, that He might sanctify and cleanse
> her with the washing of water by the word.
>
> —EPHESIANS 5:25–26

> You are already clean because of the word which I
> have spoken to you.
>
> —JOHN 15:3

In this scripture in John, Jesus was speaking as the Word made flesh. Thus He was always speaking as the Word— the living Word or the written Word. There is still another and almost unexpected aspect to obtaining the cleansing property of salt for ourselves. We discover this aspect in the middle of an object lesson being taught by Jesus to the Pharisees:

> Then the Lord said to him, "Now you Pharisees make
> the outside of the cup and dish clean, but your inward
> part is full of greed and wickedness. Foolish ones! Did
> not He who made the outside make the inside also?
> But rather give alms of such things as you have; then
> indeed all things are clean to you."
>
> —LUKE 11:39–41

In the very next verse, Jesus went on to say that they certainly did give their tithes, giving down to the tiniest detail and smallest portions. Isn't tithing giving? Of course it is. Yet He still accused them of being full of greed on the inside, because He knew their hearts were not liberated and freely giving to God or others. What they were giving was by the letter of the law, which kills, bringing death instead of life.

> Not that we are sufficient of ourselves to think of anything as being from ourselves, but our sufficiency is from God, who also made us sufficient as ministers of the new covenant, not of the letter but of the Spirit; for the letter kills, but the Spirit gives life.
> —2 CORINTHIANS 3:5–6

So what was the necessary remedy He gave to them for cleansing themselves of greed and selfishness? A rather surprising remedy in light of the fact that they were already giving everything in their tithing. But their problem was the restriction of the heart—they were not able to surrender anything beyond what was needed to be "precisely right" with God. In our present-day vernacular, we would say they gave only what they had to give to be "politically correct" with God.

So what solution did our Lord offer them? He told them all things would indeed be clean if they could give of themselves cheerfully, from the heart, presenting their freely given heart-gifts of such things as they had. The Amplified Bible states it this way:

> But [dedicate your inner self and] give as donations to the poor of those things which are within [of inward righteousness] and behold, everything is purified and clean for you.
> —LUKE 11:41, AMP

The Lord says we are to cleanse ourselves of *hidden*

inner greed and selfishness by giving of ourselves to the poor and those who are in need. That means the spiritually poor who have spiritual needs as well as the physically poor who have physical needs. He tells us that it is the necessary remedy in order to procure and receive the cleansing property of salt for ourselves.

> And the King will answer and say to them, "Assuredly, I say to you, inasmuch as you did it to one of the least of these My brethren, you did it to Me."
> —MATTHEW 25:40

> But if we walk in the light as He is in the light, we have fellowship with one another, and the blood of Jesus Christ His Son cleanses us from all sin.
> —1 JOHN 1:7

There are three additional keys found in this last verse that are basic to keeping ourselves as a cleansing agent for His salt.

1. The first one is *if*. Notice how that wonderful verse starts out immediately by letting us know that cleansing is a conditional promise of God. *If* we will walk in the light as He is in the light, we will not only be able to obtain His cleansing properties, but to consistently retain them as well.

2. As we walk with Him in that light, we will receive confirmation that the cleansing is continuing by our fellowship and love with one another. Remember, with God there is never a spiritual operation without some natural manifestation of that operation.

3. From that place of light in the Spirit we will be perpetually enabled to cleanse ourselves in His blood from *every* sin. Every sin means both the *known* sins and the *unknown* sins. That is truly remarkable.

> Who can understand his errors? Cleanse me from secret faults. Keep back Your servant also from presumptuous sins; let them not have dominion over me. Then I shall be blameless, and I shall be innocent of great transgression.
> —PSALM 19:12–13

We do not have to wait until it becomes too heavy and burdensome to carry to pull each ponderous sin through His cleansing blood. He has made the astonishing provision that while we walk in His light, the cleansing—because of our increased sensitivity to repentance and forgiveness—will be immediate, instantaneous and continual. The physical manifestation of that spiritual operation will be evidenced by our close and intimate fellowship with Him and one another.

Then His *Spirit of forgiveness* will issue forth and flow out of us at all times so that no offense has a chance to lodge. Why? Because the force issuing forth from His Spirit of forgiveness will be greater than the force of any offense aimed directly at us. The greater force will always win out. What an exquisite place to be in the Spirit!

SALT PRESERVES

To learn how we attain the ingredient of God's preservative to our salt we do not have to look any further than the Word. How to obtain it can be set forth in just one or two short scriptures. Unfortunately, it cannot be achieved as quickly or as simply as it may be stated. Has anyone else noticed that the more difficult and compelling the spiritual truth is to accomplish, the fewer words God uses to state it?

> Whoever seeks to save his life will lose it, and whoever loses his life will preserve it.
> —LUKE 17:33

> Now may the God of peace Himself sanctify you completely; and may your whole spirit, soul, and body be preserved blameless at the coming of our Lord Jesus Christ.
> —1 THESSALONIANS 5:23

We could stop right there and have the crux of it (spelled "the *c-r-o-s-s* of it"). There is only one way to have this salt preservative in our lives: to keep our flesh nailed to the cross *each* day. To live *in Him* every moment of our day, thereby dying to everything except Him. Only in that continual death will we find the true freedom to preserve our own individuality, purpose and abundant life. Only by continually giving away that life will we be able to preserve it all as His salt.

> So that they should seek the Lord . . . though He is not far from each one of us; for in Him we live and move and have our being.
> —ACTS 17:27–28

The preserving element is the easiest of all to define and the hardest of all to retain. The principal reason why? Because we must be able to trust Him unto death, no matter how severe the trial, testing or circumstance.

We say we will be able to do that, but when the physical manifestation of that particular spiritual operation is called for, too many of us will be saying, "But I really didn't think

You would ask me to do *this* . . . not *that* way." These are the times when we are all being called upon to fasten our very lives on a peg in a secure place, as Isaiah prophesied and Paul and the early church affirmed:

> I will fasten him as a peg in a secure place, and he will become a glorious throne to his father's house. They will hang on him all the glory of his father's house.
> —Isaiah 22:23–24

We are finding out that trusting in the love and power of God to deliver us *His way* and in *His timing* must be *total.*

> And the Lord will deliver me from every evil work and preserve me for His heavenly kingdom. To Him be glory forever and ever. Amen!
> —2 Timothy 4:18

May the Lord give us the grace to allow His glory fire to burn that scripture into the deepest recesses of our heart. God's preservative salt is one of the clearest of His salt properties to illustrate, while at the same time being one of the most difficult to live.

Salt Seasons

Seasoning, on the other hand, is the reverse of *preserving.* It is neither obvious nor easily conveyed, even though there are numerous scriptures that illustrate the principle. But our capacity and ability to receive that seasoning element of the Lord's salt remains elusive and in direct proportion to how freely we yield ourselves to all the other properties of the Lord's salt.

If this salt of ours is to season our lives completely and wholly, it must be an inseparable part of everything we do. As we entrust and wholly commit all things to Him, He alone strengthens our ability to intensify and enhance our seasoning. Conversely, every time we spiritually default or turn unfruitful in Him, our capability to be God's seasoning is diminished.

> For everyone will be seasoned with fire, and every sacrifice will be seasoned with salt.
> —MARK 9:49

> Let your speech always be with grace, seasoned with salt, that you may know how you ought to answer each one.
> —COLOSSIANS 4:6

Those two verses sum up God's view of salt seasoning. That seasoning will affect basically every word we speak and every sacrifice we offer.

All other spiritual ingredients are combined to make up the seasoning component of our salt. Those ingredients that make the seasoning also make its flavor. Seasoning and flavor are not the same, yet one is not possible without the other. There can be no flavor without seasoning, just as there can be no seasoning without flavor. To that extent they are exclusively and mutually dependent upon one another. That is why the words *season* and *flavor* will almost always be found together in Scripture.

However, it takes more than just the assorted properties in salt for seasoning to produce its final flavor. What else is needed? That will be addressed later when we consider the sacrificial bread in which the salt is used, allowing salt to find its highest purpose.

SALT HEALS

This is the last element of salt that we will examine for now, but it is one of great importance. It is something none of us have understood to the extent or degree we should. There remains a dilemma of what we are going to do with it in the spirit. It is perhaps best exemplified by this short story in 2 Kings:

> Then the men of the city said to Elisha, "Please notice, the situation of this city is pleasant, as my lord sees; but the water is bad, and the ground barren." And he said, "Bring me a new bowl, and put salt in it." So they brought it to him. Then he went out to the source of the water, and cast in the salt there, and said, "Thus says the LORD: 'I have healed this water; from it there shall be no more death or barrenness.'" So the water remains healed to this day, according to the word of Elisha which he spoke.
>
> —2 KINGS 2:19–22

This incident becomes extraordinarily more important when it is studied symbolically and allegorically. Full revelation of the incident would wait for the spanning of centuries to His church and this dispensation. We know that the miraculous narrative did occur. But why did the Lord instruct the prophet with such peculiar and strange directives?

Could it be that this was to be a shadow and type of one of His greatest gifts to His body following Calvary? That is exactly what it was. In a duplicity of meaning He was prophetically describing an operation of the Holy Spirit that would be released and fulfilled in His church after Calvary. The original narrative needs little interpretation to see clearly that God intended this shadow and type for His church.

The men in 2 Kings 2 were obviously principal leaders of their synagogue and city, possessing great discernment and wisdom. Yet they had tried everything they knew. When all of their best efforts had failed, they knew who held the last and highest remedy. They knew to whom they had to bring their petitions.

Although many pleasant conditions and experiences had made their living there a satisfying place in the beginning, they found that even with everything else being equal, they could no longer live without the essentials that they themselves, as leaders of their people, could not supply and could not find.

In the final analysis, the contaminated water and the barren ground had eclipsed every other enjoyable, pleasurable condition in their lives. The life-giving water had become polluted and defiled. Even the ground needed for sowing had become sterile and barren because of the polluted waters.

What was God's remedy through the prophet?

First, they needed to supply the salt themselves. And they also needed to supply the new container capable of holding the salt. The people supplied what they alone could offer of what would be needed.

Then the prophet took what the people had given him and provided the lasting miracle that only he and God could supply. He took the salt and the new container to the very source of the water. There he offered up the salt by casting it into the water himself. Once in the water, the salt performed the everlasting miracle, producing life-giving waters that flowed pure and clean forever.

Then the prophet prophesied, announcing the result of God's Salt Covenant promise:

> Thus says the LORD: "I have healed this water; from it there shall be no more death or barrenness." So the water remains healed to this day.
> —2 KINGS 2:21–22

This narrative is a complete and beautiful shadow and type that represents bringing ourselves as salt in a new bowl (a new creature in Him) to Jesus (the Prophet), who releases the Holy Spirit as living waters through God our Father.

We know at last where our source of clear life-giving water is and what the Prophet had to do for the healing of those waters of life for us:

> He that believeth on me, as the scripture hath said, out of his belly shall flow rivers of living water. (But this spake he of the Spirit, which they that believe on him should receive: for the Holy Ghost was not yet given, because that Jesus was not yet glorified.)
> —JOHN 7:38–39, KJV

We have missed a great deal by not understanding this Salt Covenant with our God. He is bringing us all back to the Mark 9:49 place in life where everyone is being seasoned with fire and every *sacrifice* is being *seasoned with salt*.

The last two characteristics of salt to be examined pertain to the certainty that every one of the elements already listed and explored do two things: They *penetrate* and they *enhance*. These two properties stand as an endowment to every other individual ingredient of salt that we keep active. Each will penetrate, and each will enhance.

According to the second chapter of Leviticus there were five things—there is God's grace number *five* again—necessary in the making and providing of the sacrificial bread and grain offering that we know to be the shadow and type of Jesus Christ as God's Bread of Life:

- Unleavened flour finely ground from grain
- Oil for the priestly anointing of the grain
- Frankincense to give its rare fragrance
- Salt for its seasoning
- Fire to prepare it and release its fragrance and flavor

> The rest of the grain offering shall be Aaron's and his
> sons'. It is most holy of the offerings to the LORD
> made by fire.
>
> —LEVITICUS 2:3

Is there any way to overestimate the significance and magnitude of the covenant of salt in our lives during these countdown years? Or its importance as an essential ingredient in our grain offering and our bread? It is strenuously doubted. Has there been a great underestimating of its importance in our lives? Most assuredly.

The neglect of our Salt Covenant is just one more reason why the Lord is taking His body back to foundational principles of His teachings. Principles that we learned as part of our first joyous works and years of walking with Him. So plain and so familiar, yet so strayed from while searching for more "profound" and "deeper" truths.

The love of God is once again sending His glory fire to renew and restore us as His salt of the earth, purifying and cleansing us with His fire by His Holy Spirit for His greater anointing.

He is seasoning and maturing each one of us—penetrating both soul and heart to heal and enhance every yielded life—thereby preserving His fruit of the Spirit in us unto His coming. He is restoring the savor and the flavor to tasteless salt in those who desire it enough to yield to His glory fire to purify and cleanse.

If you will reread that last paragraph, you will find that all eight characteristics of our spiritual salt have again been listed. Only this time they are listed to identify the spiritual objectives of God's salt covenant for His body in:

- Purifying
- Cleansing
- Preserving
- Enhancing
- Seasoning
- Penetrating
- Healing
- Flavoring

These eight objectives occur in each and every life His salt touches. God's number *eight* means "new beginnings." He is giving all of us a new impetus and a new incentive for renewing our Salt Covenant with Him.

This Salt Covenant is an essential factor in God's basic restoration of all things. He is presenting us with a deeper understanding of the Salt Covenant in order to season and flavor His Bread of Life for His children all around the world. And He is stirring up our minds to remember what the Lord and Paul have already spoken to us.

> Salt is good, but if the salt loses its flavor, how will you season it? Have salt in yourselves, and have peace with one another.
>
> —MARK 9:50

> Let your speech always be with grace, seasoned with salt, that you may know how you ought to answer each one.
>
> —COLOSSIANS 4:6

Three things become evident from these last two scriptures:

1. Each one of us is individually responsible for obtaining and keeping the spiritual properties of salt in our lives by means of the gospel and the Bread of Life within us.

2. It is not to be reserved for our own gratification alone, but consistently given and supplied to others.

3. Grace and peace are required prerequisites if our salt and our speech are to be effective.

The Lord is making known His promised provision for *hidden* manna as we overcome. As we continue to follow His pillar of fire He will give us more than enough hidden manna to be our Bread of Life for the charted journey into His glorious presence.

> Your fathers ate the manna in the wilderness, and are dead. This is the bread which comes down from heaven, that one may eat of it and not die.
>
> —JOHN 6:49–50

> He who has an ear to hear, let him hear what the Spirit says to the churches. To him who overcomes I will give some of the hidden manna to eat.
>
> —REVELATION 2:17

*The tongue is a fire, a world of iniq-
uity . . . But no man can tame the tongue.
It is an unruly evil, full of deadly poison.*

—JAMES 3:6, 8

6

The Flaming Tongue

Mankind's antithesis of death or life in the power of the tongue is transparent and unmistakable:

> But His word was in my heart like a burning fire shut up in my bones.
> —JEREMIAH 20:9

> "Is not My word like a fire?" says the LORD.
> —JEREMIAH 23:29

The *adversary* of our souls continuously authors death and eternal destruction while the *Advocate* of our souls continuously authors life and eternal glory.

It was Satan's counterfeit fire that branded the tongue of fallen man as degenerate, corrupt and deadly. Because of the Fall, man's tongue became Satan's firebrand from hell. To overturn Satan's death hold on the tongue required nothing less than God's ultimate sacrificial plan.

Yet, have we ever really stopped long enough to ask why it took that ultimate sacrificial act from the Father and His only begotten Son? Would not something less have sufficed? NO!

Only Jesus, *the Word* made flesh, could bring God's redemptive restoration to man's corrupted tongue.

Whose control is behind our tongue and words today? That still depends upon what creative power source is operative. From the very beginning God gave His people clues as to why, what and how His remedy for man's corrupted tongue would be accomplished. Through prophets such as Jeremiah He spoke of how His consuming fire of glory would start by igniting His words into the inner heart of man. Jesus presented God's unchangeable foundational principle this way:

> A good man out of the good treasure of his heart brings forth good; and an evil man out of the evil treasure of his heart brings forth evil. For out of the abundance of the heart his mouth speaks.
> —LUKE 6:45

> But I say to you that for every idle word men may speak, they will give account of it in the day of judgment. For by your words you will be justified, and by your words you will be condemned.
> —MATTHEW 12:36–37

The apostle James learned this vital truth well from his Lord and half-brother. Just how thoroughly he understood and perceived this essential principle is evidenced by the rich and various ways in which God's words resound throughout James' writings. Nowhere is that more apparent than in the third chapter of James.

> For we all stumble in many things. If anyone does not

stumble in word, he is a perfect man, able also to bridle the whole body. . . . And the tongue is a fire, a world of iniquity. The tongue is so set among our members that it defiles the whole body, and sets on fire the course of nature; and it is set on fire by hell. . . . But no man can tame the tongue. It is an unruly evil, full of deadly poison.

—JAMES 3:2, 6, 8

None of the Old Testament prophets knew the evil of the tongue better than did Isaiah. He had been chosen by God to receive and proclaim more of God's messianic prophecies than any other prophet. Yet even he could not comprehend how infused he was with the iniquity of his tongue and the words of his mouth until he was in the presence and the glory of the Almighty, the Holy One of Israel, the Lord of Hosts, the King of all the ages.

So I said: "Woe is me, for I am undone! Because I am a man of unclean lips, and I dwell in the midst of a people of unclean lips; for my eyes have seen the King, the LORD of hosts." Then one of the seraphim flew to me, having in his hand a live coal which he had taken with tongs from the altar. And he touched my mouth with it, and said: "Behold, this has touched your lips; your iniquity is taken away, and your sin purged."

—ISAIAH 6:5–7

When the prophet actually beheld the pure, holy presence and glory of God, the only words he was able to utter would cite the uncleanness that issued forth out of his own mouth and lips, and that of his people. We are perhaps just now beginning to realize why God gave one remedy—and only one remedy—to Isaiah for what he had seen.

Isaiah's dilemma and God's rectifying cure would eventually, and from the same necessity, include all who would come to the Lord in His dispensational fullness of time. But the sovereign remedy would be set forth first with Isaiah, afterward being confirmed with Jeremiah and others.

God's antitoxin for Satan's toxin was to cleanse and purge mankind's lips and tongue by His consuming fire. The Genesis story over the control of man's tongue is one of the great classic encounters between God and Satan. Satan's hold over man's tongue would bring an earth-changing climax and crisis to mankind. It is described in the eleventh chapter of Genesis.

Fallen mankind possessed an unequaled singleness of purpose due to one thing alone: They had a single language in common with which to communicate, bringing them into a total unity and agreement as a result of their complete understanding of one another.

That total understanding and comprehension of one another because of their one common language had made their singularity of purpose exceptional for the processing of knowledge and intelligence. It was that one factor alone—their one common language—that made it possible for them to agree on any single purpose as one.

> Now the whole earth had one language and one speech.
>
> —GENESIS 11:1

In the strength of that unity and oneness they knew that they could accomplish any and all things upon which they had agreed. And what they had agreed upon in that unity and powerful singleness of purpose was to build an access reaching directly into heaven.

The most astonishing claim in this whole account in Genesis, however, is given by God as He responded to what He had seen and heard. He said that they would indeed be able to do exactly that!

> And the LORD said, "Indeed the people are one and they all have one language, and this is what they begin to do; now *nothing* that they propose to do will be withheld from them."
>
> —GENESIS 11:6, EMPHASIS ADDED

Why would He say, "Now nothing that they propose to do will be withheld from them"? Why couldn't He withhold it from them? He was the almighty God. Surely He could withhold anything He chose to hold back. What was the principle in this Genesis narrative that even God Almighty would not violate? What was it about these people and their circumstance and situation that placed God in a position where He was constrained and bound to honor whatever it was they were doing?

The answer to those questions is extremely important and eternally significant. It goes without restating that mankind was created in God's image. But what we tend to forget is that He freely chose to impart His own all-powerful supernatural laws of the Spirit to govern that creation.

The creative power principles of God Almighty had been irreversibly imparted with His own *Zoe* life containing His sovereign powers to create. When He breathed the breath of life into man's nostrils, that creative power source had been unalterably passed to mankind.

The freedom to choose was an inseparable part of God's impartation to man, together with His creative power principles for dominion and authority. In that one breath He had irretrievably passed on those creative powers of life to empower the life He had created a little lower than the angels and *Elohiym* Himself. (See Hebrews 2:7; Psalm 8:5.)

He had freely chosen to breathe His own creative power principles into man, knowing it would give him the choice to obey and remain in God's undefiled state, or to transgress and fall into a degenerate state. That freedom to choose was a part of the priceless gift of life He breathed into man.

Regardless of which choice man made, however, God could not deny mankind those creative power principles without denying Himself. He would also be denying the very purpose for which He created man: to have the supernatural ability to commune with His own creation—the only creation He would ever create in His own image.

Rather than having such power—now corrupt and degenerate—and living forever, He limited the time on earth that they would possess His creative power, and He confused their ability to be in unity concerning it. He was the almighty God; He could have chosen *anything* as His power source for creating when He created *all* things in the heavens and the earth.

He could have chosen silence as His source, accomplishing all of the creating of His universe by perfect silence. But He didn't.

He could have chosen thought as His creative source, merely thinking the world into existence. But He didn't.

He could have chosen winking, or the crooking of a little finger, or the pulling of one ear—or anything else—from His limitless possibilities. But He didn't.

God's creative power source is as clear as it is profound: His creative power source is His spoken word. What pleased Him was to release His awesome limitless power through the spoken word.

The Father knew before the beginning of time that He would send His Son as the Word made flesh in order to communicate directly with His people. Jesus Christ is the embodiment of God's eternal creative power source. He is holding us and all things together by the creative power of His words:

> God, who at various times and in various ways spoke
> in time past to the fathers by the prophets, has in
> these last days spoken to us by His Son, whom He has
> appointed heir of all things, through whom also He

made the worlds; who being the brightness of His glory and the express image of His person, and upholding *all* things by the *word* of His power . . .
—HEBREWS 1:1–3, EMPHASIS ADDED

The Amplified Bible puts it this way:

. . . upholding and maintaining and guiding and propelling the universe by His mighty word of power . . .

No wonder God chose the Word as the source of His creative power. Now let's go back and look one more time at what God said when He saw what fallen man was doing in Genesis. Let's take a second look at His response.

And the Lord said, Behold, they are one people and they have all one language; and this is only the beginning of what they will do, and now nothing they have imagined they can do will be impossible to them.
—GENESIS 11:6, AMP

Look again at what the last part says: " . . . now *nothing* they have imagined they can do will be impossible to them" (emphasis added). Does that sound unusually and uniquely familiar?

Haven't we seen or known of some other place in the Bible where there is that very same spiritual principle of agreement with spoken words? Didn't Jesus portray that same creative power principle to His disciples as a part of His foundation teaching in Matthew?

You will *say* to this mountain, "Move from here to there," and it will move; and *nothing* will be impossible for you.
—MATTHEW 17:20, EMPHASIS ADDED

There have always been only two requirements for

God's principle of His creative power source to be activated. Confirmation and examples of these two requirements are found in Genesis 11:6 (for fallen man) and in Matthew 17:20 (for regenerated man).

These requirements are:

- The absolute conviction to assert that what was believed and said was possible.
- The unanimity of all attesting to that assertion.

Later, in the Book of Acts, we see this creative power source restored to its original pureness and power when the believers were all in one place and in one accord. The sacrifice of the cross had already become the resulting act of total restoration. It was necessary in order to provide God's final and eternal solution to the abuse of the spiritual principle of agreement as seen in Genesis 11:6.

> They were all with one accord in one place. And suddenly there came a sound from heaven, as of a rushing mighty wind, and it filled the whole house where they were sitting. Then there appeared to them divided tongues, as of fire, and one sat upon each of them. And they were all filled with the Holy Spirit and began to speak with other tongues, as the Spirit gave them utterance.
>
> —ACTS 2:1–4

Seven of the nine gifts of the Spirit were in frequent and literal operation all throughout the Old Testament by a select few of God's people (patriarchs, kings, prophets) as they were moved upon by the Holy Spirit. Those seven gifts are enumerated in 1 Corinthians 12.

- The word of wisdom
- Word of knowledge

- Faith
- Gifts of healings
- Working of miracles
- Prophecy
- Discerning of spirits

All seven of these gifts of the Holy Spirit are found repeatedly throughout the Old Testament. An illuminating Bible study that will involve some serious spiritual calisthenics is to look for—and identify—how many of the Holy Spirit's manifestation gifts are in operation verse by verse while reading the Bible. It will make the operation of His gifts come alive and give an increased awareness of how they are manifested in His people's lives.

Curiously enough, only seven of the nine manifestation gifts of the Holy Spirit can be found in operation *before* Jesus and His finished work at Calvary. However, there are two gifts that remained conspicuously and consistently absent all throughout the Old Testament.

In all the books of the Old Testament there is only one very veiled prophetic reference that alluded to the time when God was going to speak *directly* to His people in a different way. It becomes even more arresting when we read the conditional criteria He had established for His people before they could comprehend this messianic prophecy:

> "Whom will he teach knowledge? And whom will he make to understand the message? Those just weaned from milk? Those just drawn from the breasts? For precept must be upon precept, precept upon precept, line upon line, line upon line, here a little, there a little." For with stammering lips and another tongue He will speak to this people. To whom He said, "This is the rest with which you may cause the weary to rest," and, "This is the refreshing"; yet they would not hear.
> —Isaiah 28:9–12

The full and blood-bought price in payment of that prophecy would remain due and outstanding until Calvary. Only then would Jesus' ultimate and final payment for all nine of the gifts be poured out through the Holy Spirit on all flesh as Joel 2:28 had prophesied. Not only was God going to give all seven gifts that had previously been conferred on His chosen few, but He would also pour out on all flesh two new gifts never before given to man since God confounded and confused the languages of mankind all over the earth.

The first of His new gifts never given before the cross was the speaking with new tongues. The second gift of interpretation of tongues was a direct result of the first.

> And these signs will follow those who believe: In My name . . . they will speak with new tongues.
> —MARK 16:17

It is neither the intent nor purpose of this book to discuss or examine the subject of speaking supernaturally in other languages. That subject is still a highly contested issue more appropriately left to another time and place. Such a discussion here would only cloud and greatly obscure the search of what is, for the purpose of this book, a highly significant question to be asked and answered of God's dispensational moment in time.

Why would He exclude and withhold *only* this one gift of the Spirit throughout hundreds of centuries? And why did He continue to withhold and reserve it to the very end of the dispensation, and yet allow all the other gifts of the Holy Spirit to be in operation? And then why, when God finally did release the gift, was it first released and given as a sign through His Son—the Word made flesh? And why, in turn, did He proclaim it to be one of the representative signs of His new dispensation to all who believed in Him?

To gain some answers to these questions, Scripture

undeniably takes us back again and afresh to Genesis and the last expanse of time when all the people of the earth, all flesh, were allowed to speak in the one language for one purpose.

God would never again allow man to use His own awesome created power source in such a unity of purpose until mankind had been redeemed by Jesus Christ and washed in His blood.

Then, and only then, as His redeemed new creation and joint heirs with Him, could mankind partake once more of God's pure, miraculous and creative power source. Only one requirement remained: It must be spoken by, with and through the purity of the Holy Spirit, paid for and purchased with the blood-bought cross of Jesus Christ.

And therein, encapsulated in the heart of each one of us, is the continuing conflict that rages daily in our lives: Will the words we speak be from and by the Holy Spirit for good, or will they be from our flesh or Satan for evil? That, in turn, depends on whether we are walking in the light as He is in the light, or whether we have detoured into some darkened area of our own will and way.

That war is still raging between words that are spoken by the Holy Spirit and words that are spoken by the flesh yet unyielded to His guidance and counsel. The full intensity of Jesus' foundation words in Matthew comes back to us with great impact and force.

> But I say to you that for every idle word men may speak, they will give account of it in the day of judgment. For by your words you will be justified, and by your words you will be condemned.
> —MATTHEW 12:36–37

The word *idle* in Matthew 12:36 in the Greek means "inactive, lazy, useless, barren." In short, any word that does not carry life from the Spirit.

> It is the Spirit who gives life; the flesh profits nothing.
> The words that I speak to you are spirit, and they are
> life.
>
> —JOHN 6:63

The Pharisees' words were devoid of such life. Within the framework of the four Gospels, Jesus warned us over and over again to watch out for the leaven of the Pharisees. In the very first verse of the twelfth chapter of Luke He identified what that leaven was: *hypocrisy.*

The dictionary defines *hypocrisy* as "the result of those who appear and pretend to be something other than what they actually are." Just as in the case of the Pharisees, it takes the fiery truth of God to expose and destroy the roots of leaven that feed the hypocritical words and actions of our hearts.

> Who is this who darkens counsel by words without
> knowledge?
>
> —JOB 38:2

Whatever individual shape and form that leaven of hypocrisy has taken in our lives from the fruit of our words, the continual good news from His Word is that His glory fire is able to consume them *all* with transcendent swiftness.

All that is required is repentance, the blood of the Lamb and a renewed commitment to return to the simplicity of our first love, faithfully abiding in Him alone. We are to yield and release every aspect of our lives to Him once again, allowing His purifying consuming fire to ignite us and radiate through us in humility, repentance and forgiveness.

> . . . but, speaking the truth in love, may grow up in all
> things into Him who is the head—Christ.
>
> —EPHESIANS 4:15

That is what these last days are all about. He is growing us up in all things. He is revealing His glory fire, which, as we pass through its refining intensity, transforms us into His glorious FireBride.

Nothing shows the maturity of His church more in her submission to the lordship of Jesus Christ than does the subservience of her words to His Words.

> The word that I have spoken will judge him in the last day.
>
> —JOHN 12:48

> You are snared by the words of your mouth; you are taken by the words of your mouth.
>
> —PROVERBS 6:2

Perhaps no one captures the very crux, essence and magnitude of this in fewer words than James:

> For we all stumble in many things. If anyone does not stumble in word, he is a perfect man, able also to bridle the whole body.
>
> —JAMES 3:2

The word *perfect* in the Greek is the word *teleios*. Strong's concordance translates its meaning literally as "completeness—of full age." There is no clearer sign to watch for that indicates His church is maturing into His FireBride than by watching their verbal communication, words spoken in unity and love, without guile and without pretense.

That is also the sign and manifestation of one of God's everlasting covenants that He prophesied through Isaiah to His people:

"As for Me," says the LORD, "this is My covenant with

them: My Spirit who is upon you, and My words which I have put in your mouth, shall not depart from your mouth, nor from the mouth of your descendants, nor from the mouth of your descendants' descendants," says the LORD, "from this time and forevermore."

—ISAIAH 59:21

Death and life are in the power of the tongue.

—PROVERBS 18:21

It is no wonder that Scripture contains such uncompromising standards concerning our inherited creative power source and the exacting way with which God deals with its abuse and misuse. He continues as inflexible in dealing with it today as He did in the beginning, which is with the highest discipline possible. We will eat of the fruit and the harvest of our own creative power source—whatever it is—whether that source is of the Lord or of the flesh.

Indeed, we put bits in the horses' mouths that they may obey us, and we turn their whole body. Look also at ships: although they are so large and are driven by fierce winds, they are turned by a very small rudder wherever the pilot desires.

—JAMES 3:3–4

Paul takes up James' theme and continues with this truth:

Let no corrupt word proceed out of your mouth, but what is good for necessary edification, that it may impart grace to the hearers. And do not grieve the Holy Spirit of God, by whom you were sealed for the day of redemption. Let all bitterness, wrath, anger, clamor, and evil speaking be put away from you, with all malice. And be kind to one another, tenderhearted, forgiving one another, even as God in Christ forgave you.

—EPHESIANS 4:29–32

The spiritual framework and context in which Paul writes his powerful admonition concerning the grieving of the Holy Spirit is by no means an inattentive accident. Most of us have had occasion to use this scripture when addressing some great, weighty issue. But it has infrequently or seldom been considered and used in its original context as the Holy Spirit expressed it through Paul.

The tying together of these four verses becomes a flashing spiritual alarm signaling the dangers and consequences of our words and speech when they are not positive or productive. God cautions us as to who it is we are really in danger of grieving when we prostitute His pure purposes by our spoken words.

The Word of God has much to say about negative words. We have a marvelously positive God. He left us an example in every situation of a commandingly positive Lord and Savior. Jesus was positive about every negative opposition and force He faced, even death, leaving His joint heirs with His supreme example:

> Therefore My Father loves Me, because I lay down My life that I may take it again. No one takes it from Me, but I lay it down of Myself. I have power to lay it down, and I have power to take it again. This command I have received from My Father.
>
> —JOHN 10:17–18

As His body we have received this same commandment and commission along with how it is to be received and accomplished. Jesus already knew the two major negatives that were at work in His disciples because of the great dilemma they faced in John 14:27–28.

They felt in their hearts, just as we all have felt at times,

119

that they were facing a critical crisis from which there was no escape, that it was totally and completely unalterable. Jesus, however, instantly perceived their fearful hearts.

How did He deal with those overwhelming negative spiritual toxins that were being released because of unprecedented emotional and spiritual turmoil? He did not upbraid them. He applied God's antitoxins—the only antidote that could overcome and destroy the flesh and Satan's venom of fear and confusion that was infiltrating their very souls as they grappled with life and death.

What were those spiritual antitoxins that the Lord released to them? The penetrating power of His words spoken in the Spirit, in truth and in love. His words redirected their focus back to the promises of an eternal God who was imparting His positive character qualities of peace and rejoicing. Those antitoxins would destroy the negatives as He spoke:

> Peace I leave with you, My peace I give to you; not as the world gives do I give to you. Let not your heart be troubled, neither let it be afraid. You have heard Me say to you, "I am going away and coming back to you." If you loved Me, you would rejoice because I said, "I am going to the Father," for My Father is greater than I.
>
> —JOHN 14:27–28

God's character and His never-failing promises are represented by the fruit of the Spirit. These are the only binding antitoxins and antidote we have ever had, or will ever need, in defeating the consistent attempts by our flesh and the devil to release those lethal toxins into our minds, hearts and into the very verbal expressions of our lives.

Being the Word made flesh, He knew the timeless spiritual principle of His creative power source upon which He was acting:

For out of the abundance of the heart the mouth speaks.

—MATTHEW 12:34

Scripture has much to say about the venomous power of subversive words in our lives, and it gives us a partial list of some of the principal ones. What God has to say about them is worthy of closer examination so that we may write them upon our hearts. The hazards of not doing so are clear and their consequences unmistakable. There is not one of us who does not have a spiritual requirement and necessity to consider the ways of our heart and words and to check the toxicity level of our lives each day. Because the Lord considers this of such supreme importance to us, these nine deadly and lethal hazards to all Christians are given in their scriptural entirety below:

1. *Empty, vain words*

   Let no one deceive you with empty [vain] words, for because of these things the wrath of God comes upon the sons of disobedience.

   —EPHESIANS 5:6

2. *Persuasive, enticing words*

   Now this I say lest anyone should deceive you with persuasive [enticing] words.

   —COLOSSIANS 2:4

3. *Flattering words*

   For neither at any time did we use flattering words, as you know, nor a cloak of covetousness—God is witness.

   —1 THESSALONIANS 2:5

4. *Words to no profit*

Remind them of these things, charging them before the Lord not to strive about words to no profit, to the ruin of the hearers.

—2 TIMOTHY 2:14

5. *Great swelling words of emptiness and vanity*

For when they speak great swelling words of emptiness [vanity], they allure through the lusts of the flesh, through lewdness, the ones who have actually escaped from those who live in error.

—2 PETER 2:18

6. *Malicious words*

Therefore, if I come, I will call to mind his deeds which he does, prating against us with malicious words.

—3 JOHN 10

7. *Harsh, grievous words*

A soft answer turns away wrath, but a harsh [grievous] word stirs up anger.

—PROVERBS 15:1

8. *Words of a talebearer*

The words of a talebearer are like tasty trifles [wounds], and they go down into the inmost body.

—PROVERBS 18:8

9. *Lying words*

Also the schemes of the schemer are evil; he devises

wicked plans to destroy the poor with lying words, even when the needy speaks justice.

—Isaiah 32:7

Getting treasures by a lying tongue is the fleeting fantasy of those who seek death.

—Proverbs 21:6

These six things the Lord hates, yes, seven are an abomination to Him: A proud look, a lying tongue, hands that shed innocent blood, a heart that devises wicked plans, feet that are swift in running to evil, a false witness who speaks lies, and one who sows discord among brethren.

—Proverbs 6:16–19

The Lord's glory fire is burning toxic chaff and poison utterances out of the heart and tongue of His FireBride. Such poisons are not only without God's Spirit, but they create their own barren wasteland, sowing and carrying with them their own seeds of destruction.

Today there is little doubt that God's creative power of life and death has always resided in the power of the tongue. He has repeatedly proclaimed it to be so throughout the ages to whosoever would hear and heed.

The finished work of Jesus Christ redeemed man's creative power source. Scripture places God's life-giving words into nine basic categories. It was always His plan that our words would once again be anointed with the same life-giving power principles that He gave to His first Adam and redeemed through His last Adam.

These nine main classifications are listed in subsequent paragraphs, together with examples that reflect the categorizing found in Scripture. When spoken, these nine are anointed by God to become both pivotal and life changing. So much so that Scripture calls them "word of . . ."

WORD OF EXHORTATION

> And after the reading of the Law and the Prophets, the rulers of the synagogue sent to them, saying, "Men and brethren, if you have any word of exhortation for the people, say on."
> —ACTS 13:15

The Greek word for *exhortation* means "imploration, consultation, beseech, entreat, comfort. To invoke. To call near." Inherent in its very meaning is an almost endless array of methods and ways by which the word of exhortation is able to reach into the mind and heart of its listener with the anointed power of God's words.

Paul was unequaled for knowing and understanding where his hearers were in their life experiences before communicating his message by the word of exhortation. In his writings, he gives us a clue as to the needed wisdom of God that had been imparted to him for speaking the word of exhortation—whether it be to an individual, or to the masses, whether they be the saved or the unsaved.

> To the weak I became as weak, that I might win the weak. I have become all things to all men, that I might by all means save some. Now this I do for the gospel's sake.
> —1 CORINTHIANS 9:22–23

> And I appeal to you, brethren, bear with the word of exhortation, for I have written to you in few words.
> —HEBREWS 13:22

God watches over His word of exhortation both fervently and zealously. It is the means by which, more than any other, He guides and instructs His people. It is also one of the most continuous and effectual means by which He imparts the creative power of His spoken word.

But regardless of the great latitude God has given His church concerning the word of exhortation, there is one requirement in which He continues to be exact. That requirement is that His power source in us be kept *pure* through *prayer* and by the operation of the *fruit* and the *gifts* of the Holy Spirit.

WORD OF RECONCILIATION

The word of reconciliation is without a doubt at the very essence of God's heart, personifying His timeless mission with His creation:

> That is, that God was in Christ reconciling the world to Himself, not imputing their trespasses to them, and has committed to us the word of reconciliation. Now then, we are ambassadors for Christ, as though God were pleading through us: we implore you on Christ's behalf, be reconciled to God.
>
> —2 CORINTHIANS 5:19–20

> Leave your gift there before the altar, and go your way. First be reconciled to your brother, and then come and offer your gift.
>
> —MATTHEW 5:24

There are seven other distinct spiritual categories of "the word of . . . " to which God is taking His remnant church and FireBride back in these last days. He considers them so fundamentally essential in getting us back to His first works that they can all ultimately be tracked back to the word of exhortation or the word of reconciliation, or to some combination of both:

- Word of prophecy (2 Pet. 1:19; Rev. 19:10)

- Word of wisdom (1 Cor. 12:8)
- Word of knowledge (1 Cor. 12:8)
- Word of patience (Rev. 3:10)
- Word of righteousness (Heb. 5:13–14)
- Word of truth (2 Cor. 6:7; Eph. 1:13)
- Word of faith (Rom. 10:8)

Together these nine lay a rock-solid foundation as God's unshakeable plumb line for the structuring of His Word (Heb. 4:12; 1 Pet. 1:23, 25). His created power source will be alive and well in His FireBride.

Hearts and lips are being purged and cleansed with the holy fire of God to speak only words that will bring love and glory to His name.

> Then the LORD put forth His hand and touched my mouth, and the LORD said to me: "Behold, I have put My words in your mouth."
> —JEREMIAH 1:9

> "Is not My word like a fire?" says the LORD, "and like a hammer that breaks the rock in pieces?"
> —JEREMIAH 23:29

And you shall command the children of Israel that they bring you pure oil of pressed olives for the light, to cause the lamp to burn continually.

—Exodus 27:20

Let your waist be girded and your lamps burning.

—Luke 12:35

He was the burning and shining lamp, and you were willing for a time to rejoice in his light.

—John 5:35

7

The Road to Burning

This is the time of intense spiritual polarities: Gross darkness is growing darker in direct proportion to the radiant light of Christ growing brighter. God is fulfilling His prophesies and promises in the very midst of increased enemy persecution fighting against those prophesies and promises. The Lord is imparting more of His character and power concurrently with the increase of the spirit of antichrist with Satan's lying deceptions.

Because of these increasing polarities there are multiplied pressures that produce multifaceted crises. It is a time when we are surrounded by all of the scriptural signs of this dispensation's final nightfall. A night such as we, or the world, have never known. A night of great wilderness and deserts.

> Then His disciples said to Him, "Where could we get enough bread in the wilderness to fill such a great multitude?"
>
> —MATTHEW 15:33

It is the time when His people are once again hungry in wilderness places and desolate areas. The disciples had always looked to the Lord to provide their needs. Now He was telling them not only to feed themselves, but to provide for the multitude. They did not understand that He was taking them to a new and higher place in the Spirit. And like every new, higher place in the Spirit, it appeared almost beyond their comprehension, let alone their achieving.

We, like those disciples, are looking at Him perplexed and more than a little overwhelmed, exclaiming, "But we are suffering hunger pangs ourselves. Where do we get enough bread in this wilderness to feed ourselves and all those who are hungry around us?" Yet the Lord is instructing each of us much as He did His early disciples that we do precisely that.

Not since the days of the earliest church has there been such intense fiery extremes, combined with seemingly impossible love mandates from our Lord. During this time we do not need more formulas to accomplish what in the natural appears to be unattainable. Nor do we need more opinions. We do not even need more guidelines on how to fight or pray. More than anything else we need what the early church needed.

We need to find the presence and wisdom of God!

If we are to be successful in following His pillar of fire to glory, completing our journey, it will be because we have not only found, but have *entered into* that consuming burning presence of His love. However, if we fail to seek that continual presence, the fires from *both sides* will become too hot for every aspect of our lives that attempts to survive in a fleshly domain.

But the ultimate question is: How do we find that fervent, burning and abiding presence to walk with Him *continually?* All of the old commitments and ways by which we were once able to obtain that burning presence have increasingly failed in light of the magnitude of God's power, peace and presence now being required.

Our whole heart and soul hungers and thirsts in the birthing preparation for more of God and His presence. These are the laboring, struggling and extremely difficult birthing pains being experienced by His remnant church today.

> For we know that the whole creation groans and labors with birth pangs together until now. Not only that, but we also who have the firstfruits of the Spirit, even we ourselves groan within ourselves, eagerly waiting for the adoption, the redemption of our body.
> —ROMANS 8:22–23

This is very analogous to the struggling birth pains that were being experienced by the early church as the two disciples set out on their journey down the Emmaus road. The Emmaus experience is given to us as a forerunning prophetic example of how the Lord purposes to examine and test the spiritual foundations of our walk before, during and after extreme trials of our faith. It becomes paramount and more than worth our while to take another and closer look at the familiar incident from a different spiritual perspective.

The period during which this Emmaus lesson of the Lord's unfolds was an extremely painful crisis time for the early church, with great testing and ultimate discouragement. While He remained with them, all of the Lord's words and promises had been believed. They knew and believed they were destined to partake in a glorious and electrifying victory. Now after His death it all had become a tragic delusion to them.

For three and a half years they had walked in that wonderful fiery presence as aspirations and faith flamed through all that they heard and did. They had believed that *nothing* was impossible to them. Now they had lost that presence, and along with it their joy, their burning passions and their promises of overcoming victory.

> And their words seemed to them like idle tales, and they did not believe them.
>
> —LUKE 24:11

When we trace the Greek word *Emmaus* back to its original meaning, we find an unusual and unused root, which literally means "to be hot from sunrise to sunset." In other words, to be perpetually, continually hot and burning.

It becomes important to retrace their steps on that journey in order to examine their natural and spiritual states of mind, as well as their emotions. It will give us the needed insights into His guidance of our footsteps as we now make our own personal Emmaus journey—a journey and destination that the Lord intends for us to make and complete victoriously if we are to fervently burn for Him again in these last days. It will be a glorious and passionate return to our first love.

From the Luke 24 account we are not sure why the disciples started on their journey or what they had planned as they headed for Emmaus. It appears that they, like us, just wanted to get away from the devastating crisis of recent pressures and events—at least for a little while.

In any event, the disciples left the site of their testing, with all its pain and unfulfilled promises, not knowing how to cope with all of the massive questions assaulting their emotions and minds. His promises now seemed illusory and remote. There was great difficulty even to hold on. Great apprehensions, doubts and rationales were rampant on that road, both for themselves and their relationship with their God.

Are not the parallels all too similar and apparent when we look at the crises and difficulties of our own lives? Have we not recently—if not indeed presently—traveled that same road more than once?

We look at the sepulchers and tombs where our precious promises from God now seem to lie dead and buried under layer after layer of pressures, testings, discouragements and crises. Too often the more we attempt to walk among the seemingly forsaken promises the more there comes a growing sense of numbness and emptiness.

We began this journey, just as they did, with all the great expectations that Jesus could give us of His everlasting promises and treasures. Then slowly, we find that one treasured promise after another seemingly lay just beyond our grasp. Finally, little by little they became all too lifeless and buried amid graves of weariness, apprehensions, fears and all of the myriad violent onslaughts of the enemy.

And so we find ourselves transported on that same Emmaus journey and road that those disciples unquestionably did take—not so much toward something as away from something, away from the pressures and persecutions. However, the Lord had said through David that:

> The steps of a good man are ordered by the LORD.
> —PSALM 37:23

Unknown to the two disciples (and too often to us), *He* was the one who had ordered the journey down that lonely road from Jerusalem to Emmaus. So it was in Luke 24:13 that the disciples started walking from Jerusalem to Emmaus.

Jerusalem literally means "dual." We know the name of this city now as the *City of Peace*, because the *salem* in "Jeru*salem*" means "peace." But its literal meaning in the Hebrew is "dual." That is perhaps because it has dual and opposing meanings in Hebrew, "living of God" and "alive" vs. "raw flesh" and "repair." In David's time, Jerusalem was occupied by the enemy Canaanites. And *Canaanite* means "to bend the knees, hence to humiliate, and to bring down low."

The two disciples had started from Jerusalem alive but with their flesh raw, having a great need to be repaired and restored again and to be living in God. They needed to once again be burning in faith in Him and His promises. They had been mentally and emotionally bound by the enemy, humiliated and brought very low.

We only know the name of one of the disciples on the Emmaus road that day, and perhaps that is the only name we need to know. His name was *Cleopas*, which actually means "called of God."

And so the two disciples—*two* is God's number for *witness*—started on a journey down a road that would take them a distance of essentially seven and a half miles. Just past God's number *seven*, meaning "completeness," and right before God's number *eight*, meaning "new beginnings."

It now becomes very clear that *this Emmaus road was a road of the heart*. A road God intended them to travel down from the beginning. It was in actuality the *Lord* who was directing their every step.

He knew that in those seven and a half miles He would renew, restore, complete and bless them with a new beginning. And His new beginning would recreate hearts that could burn perpetually in faith and trust for Him.

It was God's way of victoriously transcending each step of the pilgrimage that the enemy had set for their humiliation, failure and defeat. The Lord was hidden from the eyes of the disciples but was nevertheless walking with them and beside them.

> And though the Lord gives you the bread of adversity and the water of affliction, yet your teachers will not be moved into a corner anymore, but your eyes shall see your teachers. Your ears shall hear a word behind you, saying, "This is the way, walk in it," whenever

you turn to the right hand or whenever you turn to
the left.

—Isaiah 30:20–21

So it was, while they conversed and reasoned, that
Jesus Himself drew near and went with them.

—Luke 24:15

There are some things we would do well to note here.
First, because they were communing, reasoning and fel-
lowshiping together as they walked that road, they were
fulfilling the *two spiritual requirements* necessary for Jesus to
be there in the midst of them—no matter whether they
recognized Him or not.

"Come now, and let us reason together," says the
Lord, "though your sins are like scarlet, they shall be
as white as snow."

—Isaiah 1:18

For where two or three are gathered together in My
name, I am there in the midst of them.

—Matthew 18:20

But still they didn't *know* Him. One of the most important questions in all of this should be asked of each one of
us if we are to learn from the example that is left for us by
this Emmaus journey. Why didn't they know Him? Why
didn't they recognize Him? There have been many varied
premises set forth throughout the years, but one more is
herein offered.

Their spiritual eyes had been blinded by the great crisis
in their lives. It left them apprehensive, fearful and incapable of seeing God's miraculous realm. For over three
years that realm had been made consistently visible and
real to them. But without His physical presence revealing
that spiritual realm, they could no longer envision nor

believe those truths and promises as still alive and well.

Looking at the black, dark crisis through their natural eyes quickly brought Satan's scales, which blinded their eyes of faith to God's eternal kingdom. They were no longer able to see or perceive that His promises had all been given through that incorruptible realm of the Spirit. Those promises were *all* irreversible and eternal *regardless* of what *might temporarily* occur in the natural realm.

At the time they had forfeited their ability to grasp that truth. They had just beheld and witnessed one of the most violent crises of their lives. Everything that could be shaken was being shaken. And because of the immensity of that shaking, they let the natural circumstances of what they saw and heard overshadow and obscure all of the Lord's indestructible and irreversible words and promises to them.

They had allowed enemy blows and counterfeit fires to stun and frighten them into losing their focus. They had taken their spiritual eyes off their Lord when those eyes became full of natural evidences of defeat and failure. They had obtained their experiences of faith by being taught by their Lord precept upon precept in spiritual progressions. Every advancement in the spirit realm had seemed unattainable at first, and then had become not only attainable but eagerly anticipated and followed after.

However, that was by virtue of the fact that the Lord was there with them in a physical form, helping them to make that essential transition from the natural realm to the spiritual realm. Their experiences had always included the physical body of their Lord, upon which they were able to keep their eyes focused in bridging between the two realms.

In losing their focus the disciples had lost their perspective as God set in motion the passion of the cross. He was preparing them to go far beyond their familiar experiences to discover a higher realm and greater dimension.

This crisis had blinded and rendered them incapable of recalling exhortations and admonitions given by the Lord to maintain their belief and trust *regardless* of what they experienced. Hidden in their memory was the irrevocable fact that the higher realms of the Spirit could only be achieved by keeping their spiritual eyes on Him *regardless* of what was seen, heard and experienced in the natural.

Instead, they had allowed their eyes, mind and emotions to focus on the devastation of the crisis. Their spiritual world as they had known it appeared in the natural to have been overthrown and their victory lost.

But after all, do we not go through the same governing factors today with our battles in our theater of war between the natural and spiritual focal points? When the crisis gets violent enough, don't we tend to vacillate between natural and spiritual worlds? As long as He makes Himself known in ways that are familiar to us, we are able to remain focused and keep our eyes single on Him, His Word and His promises. But when the impact of increased trials and crises come, they likewise often blind spiritual eyes and focus as we attempt to deal in the natural with the effects of the enemy's hold. We tend to lose that spiritual focus because our eyes are concentrating on all of the enemy blows taking place. In the process we remember too little of His promises because our faith has not been enlarged enough to focus on Him all the way through the crisis, *regardless*.

That kind of focused faith is freely given only by the Author and Finisher of our faith through the Holy Spirit. Moreover, that faith is absolutely essential if we are to know Him in an ever-continuing new and greater dimension. There are so many ways in which we have yet to experience and know our Lord in those larger spiritual dimensions. He lovingly contemplates showing us all of them!

For we walk by faith, not by sight.
—2 CORINTHIANS 5:7

> While we do not look at the things which are seen,
> but at the things which are not seen. For the things
> which are seen are temporary, but the things which
> are not seen are eternal.
>
> —2 CORINTHIANS 4:18

It is essential in these last days that we keep our hearts, minds and spirits continually focused on Jesus, regardless. Only then will we be able to recognize Him, regardless of the way He chooses to show Himself to us, and regardless of the severity of the circumstances.

In the midst of all our testings, discouragements, frustrations, pressures and even honest doubting we must keep Him and the unshakeable truth of His Word at the center of our very being (Mark 9:24). Only in that very center will we find His peace, which becomes the eye in the midst of all the hurricanes and storms of our lives.

However, with us—just as it was with the two disciples on the road to Emmaus—the problem becomes twofold: 1) We focus on the ordeal and the crisis with the feelings, thoughts and emotions that they invoke and extract; and 2) we allow ourselves to slip from standing solidly on the rock and the truth of His Word, which He puts above His name.

> I will worship toward Your holy temple, and praise
> Your name for Your lovingkindness and Your truth;
> for You have magnified Your word above all Your
> name.
>
> —PSALM 138:2

It is little wonder that when He comes into the midst of us we don't realize or recognize that it is He, or that He is trying to show us a way of escape. When our focus diminishes, our faith diminishes.

Our loss of faith in His ability to show us the way to total victory will be in direct proportion to our loss of focus on Jesus and His Word.

Like David, too many of us are finding out that we have not properly prepared and equipped ourselves for this new level of testing and warfare in the Spirit. Nor are we adequately prepared for the increased battle testings in the weighty armor that God has provided us.

> So Saul clothed David with his armor, and he put a bronze helmet on his head; he also clothed him with a coat of mail. David fastened his sword to his armor and tried to walk, for he had not tested them. And David said to Saul, "I cannot walk with these, for I have not tested them."
>
> —1 SAMUEL 17:38–39

The Lord has been preparing us by requiring the testing of His armor, previously enumerated in chapter three of this book. He is asking us to walk and fight in His armor on the battlefield during this night season. In that way He will be able to see how much we have actually prepared ourselves for fighting in armor in every circumstance, even the darkest ones.

There can be no continued major victorious battles in the spirit realm without daily lifting up and holding up the sacrificial weights of discipline, responsibility and accountability. Through these daily disciplines we will secure the custom fit of our armor for fighting flexibility.

Without the building up of individual spiritual muscle tone and intensity, thereby custom fitting God's armor, we will find ourselves too uncomfortable and unable to walk well in our armor—let alone to fight well or long in it. The armor soon becomes too heavy, too cumbersome, too awkward and too uncomfortable to wear and fight in continuously. This will eventually cause us to lay aside or to give back some portion of it along the way.

And the things that you have heard from me among

many witnesses, commit these to faithful men who will be able to teach others also. You therefore must endure hardship as a good soldier of Jesus Christ. No one engaged in warfare entangles himself with the affairs of this life, that he may please him who enlisted him as a soldier.

—2 TIMOTHY 2:2–4

And from the days of John the Baptist until now the kingdom of heaven suffers violence, and the violent take it by force.

—MATTHEW 11:12

The church had been given her spiritual ground rules for warfare confrontation from the beginning. But now she is being asked to progress in her preparations to the Lord's final and fervent "Green Beret" forces. Essential to that preparedness is the continual use of our armor, customizing its fit for dexterity and ease of maneuverability.

Then He said to them, "O foolish ones, and slow of heart to believe in all that the prophets have spoken! Ought not the Christ to have suffered these things and to enter into His glory?"

—LUKE 24:25–26

And they drew nigh unto the village, whither they went: and he made as though he would have gone further.

—LUKE 24:28, KJV

He is not going to impose Himself on us, even in our despair. He listens patiently and compassionately, waiting for us to call to Him from the depths of our hearts—as deep calls unto deep. He will never be satisfied with anything less than all of the real, fervent us. Not the fearful us. Not the half-hearted us. All of the real us.

But they constrained him, saying, Abide with us: for it is toward evening, and the day is far spent. And he went in to tarry with them.

—LUKE 24:29, KJV

Constrained means "to force, to compel." Remember, the violent take the kingdom by force. There is an enormous intensity to the meaning of that word *constrained*. It denotes the kind of burning fervency for which He has been waiting. It was not until that point of burning fervency had been reached that He would intervene and make the reality of His presence known to them. By that time, not coincidentally, the day was far spent and the darkness of night was quickly approaching.

When all attempts in their own understanding had been explored and found wanting, when all answers sought were seen as being denied or inadequate, when all searching seemed to lead to nothing more than another dead end, there still came a need that cried out even in the presumed emptiness with all their hearts, and all their souls, and all their strength. Their hearts were still reaching out and searching. And deep was still calling unto deep.

And *that* was what He had been waiting for in order to reveal His presence to them. His presence had already been accompanying them with every step they had taken. His voice had already spoken to them in answer to all their questions. But the thick scales of despondency, doubt, desperation and deception had closed their eyes and ears from knowing that it was Jesus walking and talking to them.

Why? *Because they were not looking for Him in the manner He chose to appear to them.*

Everything they had seen with their natural eyes was shouting "defeated," "hopeless" and "failed" to the mind and emotions. Only one source of their being, their hearts, had not been entirely encased. But happily, that is where God has always been looking and searching.

And that is where the searching and testing were taking

place in the two disciples. He had been testing and trying their faith in the hot, intense fires of the recent crisis, allowing all the impurities to come to the surface for removal. The end result was to become far more precious than gold to Him.

Paul, using the reverse of time sequence, would echo almost the exact same words spoken in Luke 24:29 when writing to the Roman church:

> Besides this you know what [a critical] hour this is, how it is high time now for you to wake up out of your sleep (rouse to reality). For salvation (final deliverance) is nearer to us now than when we first believed. . . . The night is far gone and the day is almost here. Let us then drop (fling away) the works and deeds of darkness and put on the [full] armor of light.
> —ROMANS 13:11–12, AMP

That is precisely where, unknowingly, the two disciples were on the Emmaus road. They were once again becoming a foreshadow and example of what the early and latter church would go through in searing testings of faith.

> Now it came to pass, as He sat at the table with them, that He took bread, blessed and broke it, and gave it to them. Then their eyes were opened and they knew Him. . . . So they rose up that very hour and returned to Jerusalem, and found the eleven and those who were with them gathered together . . . and they told about the things that had happened on the road, and how He was known to them in the breaking of bread.
> —LUKE 24:30–31, 33, 35

These are extraordinary statements in these verses from Luke 24. Why would both disciples know Him only after He had taken, blessed and broken the bread?

And why was it such a vital characteristic that they immediately communicated it again when describing to the apostles how they had come to know Him?

There have been many worthwhile suppositions presented through the years. However, the one that is presented here concerns the great shakings of God. The crucifixion was an unprecedented shaking of everything that could be shaken, which included the disciples' reactions and fears resulting from exceptional despair and turmoil regarding everything they knew and held dear in their natural world.

God had already commanded by the Spirit that everything that was not of Him was to be shaken, down to the very foundation of His kingdom. Among those things that were being tested in this great shaking were their very hearts and souls.

But how was breaking of bread exacting and powerful enough to be able to *instantly* cut through all of the dark passions of earthly events and crises?

What was it about that one enactment that would cause them to stand once more on God's unshakeable spiritual foundation of kingdom principles where they could see natural happenings through and with spiritual eyes?

Remember Matthew 15:33? The disciples had asked, "Where could we get enough bread in the wilderness to fill such a great multitude?" That miraculous incident was the act He had depicted and portrayed once again in front of them. That time in the wilderness had also been a place of overwhelming hopelessness in their ability to provide a solution. But He had asked just one thing of them in order for them to become partakers in His miraculous provisions: He asked only that they bring to Him *what*—and *all*—they had.

While they were in that natural realm, surrounded by their inadequate resources of a few loaves and fishes, He performed His miracle of profuse and exceeding abundance.

The sum total of what He asked them to do *themselves* was to gather up all their meager insufficiencies and bring them to Him. Then He took those very same insufficiencies and used them to accomplish the impossible task He had given them in feeding the multitude.

How did He do that? The same way He has *always* done it. By taking those things in the natural that stand as constant limiting reminders of our own inadequacies and impossibilities and using them as a testimony in the accomplishment of His miraculous abundance.

What spiritual principle did He initiate to accomplish so powerful an identifying miracle?

As He spoke the blessing, He imparted all the anointed essence of His very nature: His being, the Bread of Life. The Lord, as that Living Bread, was fulfilling God's sacrificial example, which the Father had assigned to the Son from the foundation of the world.

- He took Him . . .
- He blessed Him . . .
- He broke Him (1 Cor. 11:24) . . .
- He gave Him . . .

The anointed power of almighty God Himself could be felt transforming the very depths of their hearts and souls in that portrayal, although they did not yet fully understand all of the reasons.

They undoubtedly had been with Him on the mountainside that day, as well as many other times. They had watched as He, who held the very sustenance of life itself as their spiritual bread, then held up natural bread. They had watched Him take it, bless it, break it and give it as the Creator's unfathomable anointed power resident in Him and through Him exemplified the Bread of Life. It was to become the consecrated, sanctified pattern and example for all who would follow after Him.

> And they said to one another, "Did not our heart *burn* within us while He talked with us on the road, and while He opened the Scriptures to us?" So they rose up that very hour and returned to Jerusalem. . . . And He opened their understanding, that they might comprehend the Scriptures.
> —LUKE 24:32–33, 45, EMPHASIS ADDED

It is vital we learn the lessons of the Emmaus road journey. It is essential that we hear what the Lord is saying to us by the Spirit down those desolate dusty miles. They made the trip almost two thousand years ago, but we have been making that same journey again in these last days.

We too must experience the revelation anew and afresh, both of Himself and His presence as we travel the heart-and-soul miles of growing obstacles and darkness to greater glory. We have a need as well as a spiritual requirement from the Lord to meet the same two fervent criteria that the disciples first met. (See Isaiah 1:18; Matthew 18:20.)

We need to open up our searching hearts and minds both to one another and to Him in the midst of every burning crisis. It will be of no small consequence if we do not listen and learn what the Spirit is saying through their journey and on our own Emmaus roads.

1. He is saying that the very things that bring the intensity of the testings are the things that will bring the greater anointing and make manifest more of the presence and the glory of God in our lives.

2. He is saying that our lifeless visions, dreams and promises, lying dead in the sepulchers and tombs of our lives, are only temporarily allowed to be there for the purpose of testing and proving our trust and faith in Him and His resurrection power. He will bring them—resurrected,

145

restored and renewed—to total fruition and ful-fillment.

3. He is saying that it is only the magnified burning intensity of the crisis that produces a fiery fervor that creates our increased ability to recognize Him, His presence and His peace on an ever-higher and unshakeable level in the Spirit.

4. He is saying that in direct proportion to the intensity of the crisis and battle will come the greatness and completeness of the victory. The greater the battle, the greater the victory!

There is one all-important, unerring, ever-present covenant truth that a faithful, loving God has commanded us by His blood to remember. It is the one singular, enduring, unchangeable truth that cost Him everything. It is the one thing that He relentlessly plans and purposes for His church as joint heirs of His kingdom. It is the only thing He had in His mind, on His heart and engraved on the palms of His hands. It is what He has charged and commanded each one of us to *know* and *remember* as we go through all the Emmaus journeys of our own life:

> For I know the thoughts that I think toward you, says the LORD, thoughts of peace and not of evil, to give you a future and a hope [an expected end]. Then you will call upon Me and go and pray to Me, and I will listen to you. And you will seek Me and find Me, when you search for Me with all your heart.
> —JEREMIAH 29:11–13

I stood between the LORD and you at that time, to declare to you the word of the LORD; for you were afraid because of the fire, and you did not go up the mountain.

—DEUTERONOMY 5:5

Fire and hail, snow and clouds; stormy wind, fulfilling His word...

—PSALM 148:8

"Is not My word like a fire?" says the LORD.

—JEREMIAH 23:29

In this you greatly rejoice, though now for a little while, if need be, you have been grieved by various trials, that the genuineness of your faith, being much more precious than gold that perishes, though it is tested by fire, may be found to praise, honor, and glory at the revelation of Jesus Christ.

—1 PETER 1:6–7

Beloved, do not think it strange concerning the fiery trial which is to try you, as though some strange thing happened to you; but rejoice to the extent that you partake of Christ's sufferings, that when His glory is revealed, you may also be glad with exceeding joy.

—1 PETER 4:12–13

...rejoicing in hope, patient in tribulation, continuing steadfastly in prayer.

—ROMANS 12:12

We are traveling one last time along those same spiritual and emotional seven and a half miles. We have completed the first phase of our adolescent-to-adult walk with Christ where we found Him usually not too far away for too long at a time in the heat of the battles. Our "Jerusalem" was pretty much His home base, and although we would not see Him for short periods of time, we could still "sense"

He was there. And when the battles would get too prolonged, we had only to spend a little more time praying and calling on Him before He returned.

But this is the final hour in which He will require us to start once more with the basic fundamentals required for a new beginning on His firm foundation alone. He is forging His church's maturity, using these fiery castings to form and shape all of the radiant and glorious features for the appearance of His bride—His glorious FireBride!

It is of greatest importance that we have our foundation firm and solid in the Spirit for our final new beginnings on the rock. Without it, it will be extremely difficult—if not impossible—to seek Him and to keep on seeking Him if our hearts are not burning with equal intensity.

> So I say to you, ask, and it will be given to you; seek,
> and you will find; knock, and it will be opened to you.
> —LUKE 11:9

The words *ask*, *seek* and *knock* are words that in the original Greek mean "to ask and keep on asking; to seek and keep on seeking; to knock and keep on knocking."

Our Lord has an unsettling tendency to appear and then vanish in lives without notice and with extraordinary swiftness. Remember what happened to the disciples immediately after their eyes were opened?

> Then their eyes were opened and they knew Him; and
> He vanished from their sight.
> —LUKE 24:31

> Now as they said these things, Jesus Himself stood in
> the midst of them, and said to them, "Peace to you."
> —LUKE 24:36

> I opened for my beloved, but my beloved had turned

away and was gone. My heart leaped up when he spoke. I sought him, but I could not find him; I called him, but he gave me no answer.

—SONG OF SOLOMON 5:6

Why does He do that to us? Why? Because He yearns for us to know that He is not doing it *to us*, but rather that He is doing it *for us*. He simply asks, How else are we to learn to walk by faith and not by sight?

While the *why* can be readily answered, the answer as to the *how*, unfortunately, cannot.

The Word, however, does provide us with the location of where this journey will ultimately lead. Surrounded by the world's ever-growing darkness, we will only be able to reach that spiritual site by His pillar of fire. As we do, He will be able to lead us to the greatest of intimacies. He will lead us into His wedding chamber. That location and the reasons why it was chosen by God will be examined in the next chapter. In the meantime:

Behold, he stands behind the wall of our house, he looks in through the windows, he glances through the lattice.

—SONG OF SOLOMON 2:9, AMP

O God, You are my God; early will I seek You; my soul thirsts for You; my flesh longs for You in a dry and thirsty land where there is no water.

—PSALM 63:1

For the LORD your God has blessed you in all the work of your hand. He knows your trudging [walking] through this great wilderness.

—DEUTERONOMY 2:7

He turns a wilderness into pools of water, and dry land into watersprings.

—PSALM 107:35

For the LORD will comfort Zion, He will comfort all her waste places; He will make her wilderness like Eden, and her desert like the garden of the LORD; joy and gladness will be found in it, thanksgiving and the voice of melody.

—ISAIAH 51:3

8

The Blazing
Desert Wilderness

In this final phase of preparation before the gathering of His FireBride unto Himself, the Lord will know her—in that most intimate sense of the word—by her fervent love, her absolute surrender and her total trust and faith in Him. She will be able to honestly rejoice and give thanks, not because of where she is in the searing desert wilderness experiences, but because of who He is to her.

These are the mature qualities being fashioned and sought by the Bridegroom's compelling desire to impart to her the very essence of His nature and character through the anointing of the Holy Spirit and His fruit.

> Many will say to Me in that day, "Lord, Lord, have we not prophesied in Your name, cast out demons in Your name, and done many wonders in Your name?" And then I will declare to them, "I never knew you; depart from Me, you who practice lawlessness [iniquity]!"
> —MATTHEW 7:22–23

> Then Jesus said to him, "Unless you people see signs
> and wonders, you will by no means believe."
>
> —JOHN 4:48

The gifts and callings of God are irrevocable and without repentance (Rom. 11:29). Because of this, He has had great and prolonged patience with us as we have followed long after these gifts, pursuing them with great excitement to see and experience all nine of the manifestation gifts of the Holy Spirit.

It seems we have been particularly absorbed in following after the word of knowledge, discerning of spirits, prophecy and the working of miracles. God has been extremely patient, giving us a window of time, characterized by decades, to examine, learn and apply these gifts, allowing us to pursue them freely.

We have watched, almost insatiably, all of those who move with great proficiency in His gifts. The body of Christ has partaken in and sought out these gifts again and again, year after year, decade after decade, with all the excitement and enthusiasm of attending and watching some great celestial entertainment attraction, enthralled by the enjoyment and self-gratification of feeling and seeing the power of God's anointing.

He has continued in great patience as we attended one conference after another, seeking yet another word from the Lord. All too often the seeking of *a word* became the pursuit—rather than the seeking of *His face, His character* and *the whole Word of God.*

The Lord again patiently waited as His body continued to seek the personal receiving of prophecy—or the personal giving of prophecy—encountering all the gifts and exercising them on one another instead of on a lost world.

For the past three or four decades the Lord has allowed members of His body to major in His awesome power gifts with great excitement and fascination. Many in His body have become increasingly unbalanced between His power gifts and His character fruit of the Spirit. During a growing time period there has been little sign of that maturity, so essential and indispensable for His bride.

Participants within the body of Christ may have changed from one decade to the next, but not the spiritual agenda or aptness toward maturing. The Lord has allowed us this enormous time and freedom in exercising His power gifts so that the church would master all of God's spiritual curricula, adding precept upon precept, and accomplishing them for that one ultimate purpose: to give back out to His lost and dying world.

But for decades we have chosen to take everything in and to give out very little, thinking that the more we took in the faster we would mature. So we took in and took in and took in. And then we took in some more. We are now finding there are many grievous and abusive things wrong with that.

At first, we were just so hungry and busy taking everything in that we simply forgot at times. In spite of good intentions, we simply forgot to give back and provide for a needy brother or sister and for a lost and dying world. But over time it became easier and easier to focus on us and self and all of the help we needed. The more we took in, the less full we became. And the less full we became, the more we needed to take in. A vicious cycle was started, and still, in most cases, the intent was not evil. But the enemy has claimed its principal result: that of turning inward and centering on self.

The unhealthy result has been a flourishing of mental, emotional and spiritual malnutrition and crippling. Concentrating on the resultant hurts and wounds caused by the weakened state, it has caused confusion, self-absorption, self-pitying and self-indulgence. And perhaps most dangerous of all, it has led to self-deception, resulting in a progressive inability to turn outward and minister to others' needs.

All but forgotten is the basic and simple truth of God's plan for the healing of our wounds and growing in maturity. His anointed healing power sovereignly manifests itself as His people turn their hearts *upward* to Him and then *outward* to others. That has always been God's exclusive plan and design to keep His powerful healing anointing from becoming a Dead Sea experience, with everything flowing in and no outlet from which to flow out.

This designated plan of the Lord's was established and depicted throughout the Old Testament, perfected and fulfilled through Jesus Christ, and it has been eternally ordained to be manifested through His body. The more attempts that are made to achieve our maturity through the power of His gifts, the more instability will come from the neglect of His character fruit and its development in us. Why?

First, because that has always been God's *first* priority for the maturing of His body. It will never be delegated to any other status. Second, we have a significant lack of spiritual desire in accomplishing this priority. It involves intensely disciplining and crucifying the flesh from which we tend to vacillate, especially when weighed against the excitement and enjoyment of pursuing more of His power gifts.

Such contradictions have continued as negative dynamics with too many brothers and sisters, as well as with too many of their churches. The Lord loves us enough that He is beginning to bring all of this to closure.

We must not continue to seek and major in His power gifts at the expense and neglect of His character and the fruit of the Holy Spirit. Jesus authoritatively denounced the scribes and Pharisees of His day, decrying the practice of attempting to attain one of God's attributes at the expense of another. He intended for both to be attained:

> Woe to you, scribes and Pharisees, hypocrites…you…
> have neglected the weightier matters of the law: jus-

tice and mercy and faith. These you ought to have done, without leaving the others undone.

—MATTHEW 23:23

While His church was still in the process of growing up, He winked at our ignorance and overlooked it (Acts 17:30). But He is no longer winking or overlooking. When Paul wrote to the Corinthians after his first visit, he said:

And I, brethren, when I came to you, did not come with excellence of speech or of wisdom declaring to you the testimony of God. . . . And my speech and my preaching were not with persuasive words of human wisdom, but in demonstration of the Spirit and of power, that your faith should not be in the wisdom of men but in the power of God.

—1 CORINTHIANS 2:1, 4–5

Paul was a wise master builder. When he first came to the Corinthian church he knew that they had an essentially innocent and immature need to comprehend that this was not just another man talking to them about one of their many gods. In the beginning, the only way he could effectively fulfill that need was to reach beyond their ignorance of God and their lack of spiritual development and maturity and demonstrate the power of God.

The nine manifestation gifts of the Holy Spirit have always been at the basic entry level of the believer's spiritual attainments (1 Cor. 12:8–10). God's original plan was that each of these signs would follow each believer (Mark 16:17). The Lord intended them to be a beginning place for us in the Spirit, never a stopping or camping place.

These signs are to follow every one of us supernaturally as we minister Jesus to the needs to which He directs and guides us. We are never to follow after them; they are to follow us. Paul undertook explaining and confirming this vital truth to the Corinthian church:

> However, we speak . . . not the wisdom of this age,
> nor of the rulers of this age, who are coming to
> nothing. But we speak the wisdom of God in a mys-
> tery, the hidden wisdom which God ordained before
> the ages for our glory. . . . But God has revealed them
> to us by His Spirit. For the Spirit searches all things,
> yes, the deep things of God. . . . These things we also
> speak, not in words which man's wisdom teaches but
> which the Holy Spirit teaches, comparing spiritual
> things with spiritual. . . . For "who has known the
> mind of the LORD that he may instruct Him?" But we
> have the mind of Christ.
> —1 CORINTHIANS 2:6–7, 10, 13, 16

The final perfecting of His FireBride will come as a
result of His wisdom and fruit of the Spirit being thoroughly and fully imparted to her for her maturity. His
character and fruit of the Spirit alone are the only forces
strong enough to make and manifest love's eternal changes
to hearts and minds. The bride is being conformed into the
expressed image of her Bridegroom—she will have the very
nature and character of Christ!

But the question remains: How is He going to bring into
existence that express nature and character? If we are
honest, we will acknowledge He still has an abundance of
spiritual work to impart and make manifest in all of us!

BETHANY: THE HOUSE OF THE DATE PALM

The burning Emmaus road experience contains a vital epi-
logue and an explanation, as well as a great significance,
which has been concealed in the last verses of Luke 24. If
we dig a little, we will unearth some spiritual treasure as to
how He accomplishes this with every family member of
His household of faith:

And he led them out as far as to Bethany, and he lifted

up his hands, and blessed them. And . . . while he blessed them, he was parted from them, and carried up into heaven.

—LUKE 24:50–51, KJV

Why Bethany? Of all the locations to which He could have led them before departing, why did He choose Bethany as the place to leave them? Jesus never did anything "just because" and without sovereign reasons. He had reasons for leaving the disciples—and us—at Bethany. The exploration and explanation of those reasons will lead to a hidden mystery and treasure of God's waiting to be uncovered by digging with hunger and thirst into His Word for His maturing and His meaning.

The word *Bethany* is a prime root word. In the Greek it means "date house," or "house of dates." Jesus chose this *house of dates* as the location site for leaving them—and us. Since we are His house, it is of major importance that we understand just where He did leave us.

Whenever the Bible speaks of the "palm tree" it is always speaking of the date palm. So He led them as far as "the house of the date palm," and He blessed them—and us—there. And He left them—and us—there. Of all the places and locations where He could have chosen, this is the place He chose. There was something of vital importance to be taught and learned here in preparation for His returning.

We know that this is the exact site He chose and desired to leave them because the Word said He did more than just show them the way: He led them there.

What was it about Bethany? What was it about that "house of the date palm"? What does He have for us to learn there that will prepare us for His return that we would not be able to learn in any other location?

1. The date palm will grow, mature and flourish naturally *only* in a desert wilderness climate. It requires a hot, dry, desert wilderness climate.

2. The desert wilderness climate is the only climate and condition that will *force* the date palm's root system down ever deeper and deeper—to a depth not possible in less severe or demanding climates.

3. The date palm's endurance and survival in that environment requires that it continue to reach deeper and deeper beyond the surface to find in those depths its continuing hidden water supply source.

4. It takes many years for the date palm tree to mature enough to bear fruit—at least six to ten years after planting.

5. Once the date palm becomes mature enough to bear fruit, it increasingly produces and provides fruit without ceasing all the rest of its life.

6. The date palm tree is one of the few trees on earth for which every portion of the tree becomes usable upon maturity.

7. From the beginning of His Word in Exodus, God has shown by example how He has used the date palm as a symbol and as an epitome for and of His people.

> Then they came to Elim, where there were twelve wells of water and seventy palm trees; so they camped there by the waters.
> —EXODUS 15:27

What an explicit and beautiful analogy of the twelve apostles and the seventy disciples as they lived encamped around

Jesus—the Living Water of God. The Scriptures give us hundreds of these graphic examples of how God uses the date palm to describe qualities and virtues that are desired and required of His people, such as the one in 1 Kings:

> Then he carved all the walls of the temple all around, both the inner and outer sanctuaries, with carved figures of cherubim, palm trees, and open flowers.
> —1 KINGS 6:29

These date palm trees were carved to represent the total commitment required by God of His people. They were His symbol that the people were to grow—thrive and flourish—even in the most adverse and severe surroundings and conditions. They would be able to send their roots down deeper and deeper until they found the very source of their Living Water supply. There in that hot, dry desert wilderness they would not only be able to survive, they would be able to *flourish!*

The Lord also had these date palms carved individually, even though they stood together. This was a reminder to His people that ultimately each person is individually responsible for leading a godly life, sending our own roots down deep enough to obtain the Living Water supply. In these last days we cannot afford to be influenced by the indifference of others—or by the apathy, rebellion, criticism or discouragement of others.

David sums it up succinctly and beautifully without reservation and without exception:

> The righteous shall flourish like a palm tree.
> —PSALM 92:12

There are *two* different spiritual wildernesses that must be conquered in our own lives. They lie on either side of our spiritual Jordan River. There is, of course, the vast wilderness and desert that Moses knew and that the Israelites had to cross in order to reach the river. But we have almost forgotten there still remained a second vast wilderness and desert to be dealt with on the *other* side of the Jordan—the one that lay *within* the Promised Land.

This is the wilderness that Jesus as our example knew as the location chosen by God to be the site of great testings and Satan's temptations. This is the place where the Lord learned deep solitude and sustaining, surrendering prayer to the Father. This is the place where He was initially led by the Holy Spirit just as Jesus led us to Bethany (Matt. 4:1; Luke 4:1).

We are walking in His footsteps on the same side of the Promised Land in which He walked and lived, as well as walking out a second fulfillment of the prophetic scriptures of Moses' desert wilderness.

Having for the most part understood the first crossing of wilderness into the Promised Land, we now have a need to understand more completely God's reasons for this second wilderness and desert—the one that Jesus traveled and knew so intimately inside the Promised Land itself. The one we also have been called upon to travel and know. The one He blessed us and left us with at Bethany.

> The voice of one crying in the wilderness: "Prepare the way of the LORD; make straight in the desert a highway for our God."
> —ISAIAH 40:3

> I am "the voice of one crying in the wilderness: 'Make straight the way of the LORD,'" as the prophet Isaiah said.
> —JOHN 1:23

Certainly John the Baptist's journeys and abiding in the wilderness were an indivisible part of God's Promised Land, both spiritually and naturally. John the Baptist and the Lord are supreme examples of how God's chosen "date palms" are to flourish in righteousness even during the most severe of wilderness desert times.

> Then Jesus, being filled with the Holy Spirit, returned from the Jordan and was led by the Spirit into the wilderness.
>
> —LUKE 4:1

> So He Himself often withdrew into the wilderness and prayed.
>
> —LUKE 5:16

> He found him in a desert land and in the wasteland, a howling wilderness; He encircled him, He instructed him, He kept him as the apple of His eye.
>
> —DEUTERONOMY 32:10

> And I will bring you into the wilderness of the peoples, and there I will plead My case with you face to face.
>
> —EZEKIEL 20:35

> I knew you in the wilderness, in the land of great drought.
>
> —HOSEA 13:5

He is guiding and instructing us from the midst of His glory fire in the middle of that vast blazing wilderness as He prepares a new Garden of Eden for His FireBride after her appointed time in the desert wilderness.

> A fire devours before them, and behind them a flame burns; the land is like the Garden of Eden before them, and behind them a desolate wilderness.
>
> —JOEL 2:3

161

The Bridegroom is watching with intense longing as the bride makes herself ready (Song of Sol. 2:9).

> Let us be glad and rejoice and give Him glory, for the marriage of the Lamb has come, and His wife has made herself ready.
> —REVELATION 19:7

And how did she accomplish that? By taking every adversity and crisis as an occasion and signal to send down her spiritual roots yet deeper and deeper—beyond the hot, dry desert wilderness of trials and testings to His flowing and renewing supply of Living Water, waiting expectantly to be found in order to nourish to final maturity His FireBride residing in His house of dates.

> And He said to me, "It is done! I am the Alpha and the Omega, the Beginning and the End. I will give of the fountain of the water of life freely to him who thirsts. He who overcomes shall inherit all things, and I will be his God and He shall be My son."
> —REVELATION 21:6–7

There is only one condition to His giving of those waters freely: We must first thirst. Webster's definition of *thirst* is "to suffer thirst; to crave vehemently and urgently."

The body of Christ too often appropriates one of His *conditional* promises, claiming and standing on it as though it were one of His *unconditional* promises. Not being mindful of the conditions that God assigns to His promises too often becomes a major reason why a member of the body of Christ becomes discouraged and disillusioned.

Another example of God's conditional promises is found in verse 7 of the twenty-first chapter of Revelation: "He who overcomes shall inherit all things. . . . " The condition to that promise has literally everything riding on it. How are we going to become overcomers if there are no challenges, adversities or barriers to overcome with and by Him? Only when we live and move and have our very being in Him can we rejoice in such an absolute overcoming.

> These things I have spoken to you, that in Me you may have peace. In the world you will have tribulation; but be of good cheer, I have overcome the world.
> —JOHN 16:33

> And the Spirit and the bride say, "Come!" And let him who hears say, "Come!" And let him who thirsts come. Whoever desires, let him take the water of life freely.
> —REVELATION 22:17

When we see the FireBride of Christ first appearing in all her glory in the Song of Solomon, we see her in a very strange setting. She is resplendent in her wedding garment without spot or wrinkle. She flourishes in righteousness like a date palm. And she is leaning on her Beloved. But where has she been? From whence is she making her appearance?

If we can find the answer to that, then we will be able to confirm the site of her final preparations. We will know the location of her "dressing room"—the place where she is receiving all of the magnificent virtues and wisdom inherent in His character. We will have found the site where she is being adorned with all of His abiding honor and fruit of the Spirit. That place chosen by God for the bride to prepare for her Beloved is plainly revealed in the Song of Solomon:

> Who is this coming up *from the wilderness*, leaning on her beloved? I awakened you under the apple tree. There your mother brought you forth; there she who bore you brought you forth.
> —SONG OF SOLOMON 8:5, EMPHASIS ADDED

These words from the Song of Solomon will engrave a beautiful and unmistakable bridal portrait upon minds and hearts. That spiritual portrait would later become even more richly painted with flowing prophetic words as brush strokes and color hues of even greater depth and beauty in the second chapter of Hosea:

> "Therefore, behold, I will allure her, will bring her into the wilderness, and speak comfort to her. I will give her her vineyards [His fruit] from there, and the Valley of Achor [which means "trouble"] as a door of hope; she shall sing there, as in the days of her youth, as in the day when she come up from the land of Egypt. And it shall be, in that day," says the LORD, "that you will call Me 'My Husband,' and no longer call Me 'My Master'...
>
> "I will betroth you to Me forever; yes, I will betroth you to Me in righteousness and justice, in lovingkindness and mercy; I will betroth you to Me in faithfulness, and you shall know the LORD [the intimate relationship between husband and wife]....
>
> "The earth shall answer with grain [the Bread of Life], with new wine [the New Covenant blood of Christ], and with oil [the anointing oil of the Holy Spirit]; they shall answer Jezreel [meaning "God will sow"]. Then I will sow her for Myself in the earth, and I will have mercy on her who had not obtained mercy; then I will say to those who were not my people, 'You are My people!' And they shall say, 'You are my God!'"
>
> —HOSEA 2:14–16, 19–20, 22–23

We should have an urgency to have these verses and the message they bring joyously and indelibly written on our hearts. God fervently desires the victorious accomplishment of all our exploits while journeying through the blazing wilderness as His flourishing date palm. We should henceforth continue with the final preparations to become a resplendent bride for our Beloved and stop beholding the desert wilderness through enemy eyes.

> "The voice of joy and the voice of gladness, the voice of the bridegroom and the voice of the bride, the voice of those who will say: 'Praise the LORD of hosts, for the LORD is good, for His mercy endures forever'—and of those who will bring the sacrifice of praise into the house of the LORD. For I will cause the captives of the land to return as at the first," says the LORD.
>
> —JEREMIAH 33:11

> Blessed are those who dwell in Your house [Your house of the date palm]; they will still be praising You. Selah. Blessed is the man whose strength is in You, whose heart is set on pilgrimage. As they pass through the Valley of Baca [which means "to weep, to mourn"], they make it a spring; the rain also covers it with pools. They go from strength to strength; each one appears before God in Zion.
>
> —PSALM 84:4–7

> Who is this coming out of the wilderness like pillars of smoke, perfumed with myrrh and frankincense?
>
> —SONG OF SOLOMON 3:6

The wilderness purifies the bride.

> The words of the LORD are pure words, like silver tried in a furnace of earth, purified seven times.
>
> —PSALM 12:6

> He will sit as a refiner and a purifier of silver; He will purify the sons of Levi, and purge them as gold and

silver, that they may offer to the L ORD an offering in righteousness.

—M ALACHI 3:3

I will bring the one-third through the fire, will refine them as silver is refined, and test them as gold is tested. They will call on My name, and I will answer them. I will say, "This is My people"; and each one will say, "The L ORD is my God."

—Z ECHARIAH 13:9

The wilderness purges the bride.

Purge me with hyssop, and I shall be clean; wash me, and I shall be whiter than snow.

—P SALM 51:7

And you shall remember that the L ORD your God led you all the way these forty years in the wilderness, to humble you and test you, to know what was in your heart, whether you would keep His commandments or not.

—D EUTERONOMY 8:2

The wilderness shapes the character of Jesus Christ in His FireBride through victorious trials and testings.

Though He was a Son, yet He learned obedience by the things which He suffered.

—H EBREWS 5:8

But the God of all grace, who hath called us unto his eternal glory by Christ Jesus, after that ye have suffered a while, make you perfect, stablish, strengthen, settle you.

—1 P ETER 5:10, KJV

Therefore, since Christ suffered for us in the flesh, arm yourselves also with the same mind, for he who has suffered in the flesh has ceased from sin.

—1 PETER 4:1

If we endure, we shall also reign with Him. If we deny Him, He also will deny us.

—2 TIMOTHY 2:12

For our light affliction, which is but for a moment, is working for us a far more exceeding and eternal weight of glory.

—2 CORINTHIANS 4:17

Yes, and all who desire to live godly in Christ Jesus will suffer persecution.

—2 TIMOTHY 3:12

The desert wilderness journeys in our lives in these last days are for only two purposes: to make us *joyous overcomers* and *to reveal and make manifest His nature and character by the fruit of His Holy Spirit in us.* Then we truly can be an epistle read of all men by our words, deeds and heart motives.

We have allowed ourselves to be caught up in fighting too many of our crises and circumstances as seen through the eyes of the enemy rather than seeing through the victorious eyes of God. It has done violence to our perspective and increased our inability and ineptness at spiritually refocusing on God's glorious, joyous purposes. He desires to see His love and His purposes manifested in us.

Do you know when He gave us His joy? He gave it in the upper room as one of His last bequests at the Last Supper. He gave it when He knew the garden and the cross with their ultimate suffering and agony were already upon Him.

This things I have spoken to you, that My joy may remain in you, and that your joy may be full.

—JOHN 15:11

It was also right in the middle of His consummate prayer to the Father on our behalf. He knew we could not be overcomers without it.

> But now I come to You, and these things I speak in the world, that they may have My joy fulfilled in themselves.
>
> —JOHN 17:13

> Looking unto Jesus, the author and finisher of our faith, who for the joy that was set before Him endured the cross, despising the shame, and has sat down at the right hand of the throne of God.
>
> —HEBREWS 12:2

Jesus has patterned and embodied for us an uncompromising, resolute joy that *refuses* to bow its knee to *any* adversity because the *roots* of that joy extend all the way to the Father's throne and the River of Life. That same fountain of joy and Living Water had been foreordained to flow in us *without ceasing* when Jesus opened it up at Calvary.

That is God's joy, and it is an indivisible part of the Rock upon which we stand and are built. No turmoil, adversity or floods of affliction will be able to shake God's joy in us. That is the unconquerable joy by which we will be able to do more than just bear up and endure—that is the joy by which we will always triumph.

This is joy from almighty God, and we have inherited it! It is absolutely indispensable for our journeying in the blazing wilderness. The word *joy* and its various derivatives (such as *rejoice, joyous* and others) appear *over 388 times in the Bible.* The Lord spoke through Nehemiah with great future insight as he prophetically exclaimed an everlasting word of wisdom to God's people for their blazing wilderness journeys:

> Do not sorrow, for the joy of the LORD is your strength.
>
> —NEHEMIAH 8:10

That ability to rejoice is already in us, and He allows the strength of that joy as well as the rest of His character fruit of the Holy Spirit to *penetrate* through us until they overcome every adverse emotion and experience. That ability is critical if we are to keep an unerring focus on the victories set before us that the Lord has planned for this wilderness journey. To *know* that He is allowing the trials and adversities because He has covenanted with us to impart and strengthen another conquering spiritual facet and another aspect of His character in our lives.

We must also realize that the enemy is more than a willing adversary and has an unfailing supply and an unending abundance of attacks. He has an endless supply of great, swelling negatives and means of temptations that will attempt to:

- Anger
- Bewitch
- Charm
- Confuse
- Corrupt
- Deceive
- Disillusion
- Doubt
- Entice
- Frighten
- Lure
- Offend
- Oppress
- Profane
- Question
- Seduce
- Terrorize
- Thwart
- Weary
- Wound

And with few or no intermissions!

Never forget that Satan is a defeated brilliant strategist as well as counterfeiter. He takes one of the Lord's character traits and one of the nine fruit of the Holy Spirit, which are the main facets of that character, and attempts to destroy them in our lives—or at least render them temporarily inoperable. How in the world does he do that to us time and time again?

He does it very simply by targeting one or more of the nine fruit of the Holy Spirit in our lives, such as longsuffering. Then he attacks a behavior, conduct or reaction in that life where longsuffering is either absent, weak or has some opening to sin vulnerability.

The enemy believes he can either destroy the quality that is already there, or at least prevent it from being strengthened. The Lord allows the temptation because He has faith that we can overcome by fortifying ourselves with more of the very attribute of the Lord that Satan is trying to destroy. Whose version will we believe throughout all the blazing heat of the journey?

> Blessed is the man that endureth temptation: for when he is tried, he shall receive the crown of life, which the Lord hath promised to them that love him. Let no man say when he is tempted, I am tempted of God: for God cannot be tempted with evil, neither tempteth he any man: But every man is tempted, when he is drawn away of his own lust [desires], and enticed. Then when lust [desire] hath conceived, it bringeth forth sin: and sin, when it is finished [grown], bringeth forth death. Do not err [be deceived], my beloved brethren.
>
> —JAMES 1:12–16, KJV

The enemy is defeated and yet never gives up. Total overcoming victory has been bought and paid for by our Lord and Savior—and still we sometimes wonder if we can make it another day! No wonder the Lord is saying it is time for His church to grow up and finish maturing into His FireBride.

When the Scriptures speak of "fruit," God retains a double meaning: the fruit of souls won to Christ, and the nine fruit of the Holy Spirit. We cannot produce the fruit of souls for Christ if we do not first produce and make manifest His fruit of the Holy Spirit. While the definitions of God's two kinds of "fruit" are not the same, their inseparableness and interchangeability in His kingdom are.

> For every tree is known by its own fruit. For men do not gather figs from thorns, nor do they gather grapes from a bramble bush.
>
> —LUKE 6:44

> You did not choose Me, but I chose you and appointed you that you should go and bear fruit, and that your fruit should remain, that whatever you ask the Father in My name He may give you.
>
> —JOHN 15:16

> For the fruit of the Spirit is love, joy, peace, longsuffering, kindness, goodness, faithfulness, gentleness, self-control. Against such there is no law.
>
> —GALATIANS 5:22–23

> For the fruit of the Spirit is in all goodness, righteousness, and truth.
>
> —EPHESIANS 5:9

> By this My Father is glorified, that you bear much fruit; so you will be My disciples.
>
> —JOHN 15:8

> Now no chastening seems to be joyful for the present, but painful; nevertheless, afterward it yields the peaceable fruit of righteousness to those who have been trained by it.
>
> —HEBREWS 12:11

It should be exceptionally clear by now that we are not going to make it out of our blazing wilderness without the fruit of the Spirit and the other character attributes of our Lord. The power gifts were never meant to be enough to survive such a journey.

So what are the attributes of the nature and character of Jesus Christ that are being fashioned and forged into our lives by this time of blazing hot wilderness journeyings? And of more eternal consequence, what are the physical manifestations of the spiritual operation of these attributes that will be reflected in His FireBride? Here are just a few of the more important ones:

Boldness	Guilelessness	Longsuffering	Stability
Commitment	Honorableness	Love	Steadfastness
Compassion	Hope	Meekness	Strength
Courage	Humility	Mercy	Temperance
Diligence	Integrity	Peace	Understanding
Faithfulness	Intensity	Purity	Virtuousness
Gentleness	Joyfulness	Righteousness	Wisdom
God's beauty	Kindness	Servanthood	Zealousness
Graciousness	Knowledge		

These qualities are but representative of the Lord's limitless virtues and attributes, which His FireBride will not only possess *but manifest* consistently, reflecting His light and His express image both to one another and to the world.

If we will but center in on these in prayer every time the enemy tries to get us in a stranglehold or a counterfeit death grip, we are guaranteed to come out the victor!

Hebrews 11:6 tells us that without faith it is impossible to please God. However, Galatians 5:6 tells us how faith works: Faith works by and through *His love.*

Love never fails. But whether there are prophecies,

they will fail; whether there are tongues, they will cease; whether there is knowledge, it will vanish away. …And now abide faith, hope, love, these three; *but the greatest of these is love.*
— 1 CORINTHIANS 13:8, 13, EMPHASIS ADDED

Love is the only latchkey that will unlock every door to the nine character fruit of the Holy Spirit and to every other attribute, virtue and quality that our Bridegroom possesses.

> *Love* is the latchkey.
> *Joy* is love's song.
> *Peace* is love's shelter.
> *Longsuffering* is love's endurance.
> *Kindness (gentleness)* is love's touch.
> *Goodness* is love's nature.
> *Faithfulness (faith)* is love's strength.
> *Gentleness (meekness)* is love's tenderness.
> *Self-control (temperance)* is love's discipline.

To him who overcomes I will grant to sit with Me on My throne, as I also overcame and sat down with My Father on His throne.
— REVELATION 3:21

And they overcame him by the blood of the Lamb and by the word of their testimony, and they did not love their lives to the death.
— REVELATION 12:11

Come, I will show you the bride, the Lamb's wife.

—REVELATION 21:9

9

The Glorious FireBride

The Lord, throughout every facet of this journey, is exposing His church to one final enigma and paradox: The *only* way for the bride to move forward to final maturity in His kingdom is to go back to His never-changing foundation of basic plumb line truths and priorities. They were eternally established by Him as our unending and unalterable milestone markers for this last phase of our journey before seeing Him face to face.

He wants His FireBride to fully grasp the way that His essence as a consuming fire manifests His glory by destroying what is not of Him and refining and strengthening what is of Him—thereby fashioning all to the glory of God.

> When He comes to be glorified in His saints [on that day He will be made more glorious in His consecrated people], and [He will] be marveled at and admired [in His glory reflected] in all who have believed [who

have adhered to, trusted in, and relied on Him],
because our witnessing among you was confidently
accepted and believed [and confirmed in your lives].
—2 THESSALONIANS 1:10, AMP

It is ultimately important that we remain aware of what
He is doing and why. Also, that we understand and discern
the two polarized fires that are at work simultaneously in
our lives in the heavenlies and on earth. There is a growing
urgency in our lives as His church in the world today to
yield to His fire and allow God to forge, fashion and complete His FireBride.

A vital prerequisite for His final preparations is being
able to recognize to whose fire the bride is submitting her
members. Another prerequisite is to understand that only
God's fiery armor is capable of total and victorious protection from the growing darkness and escalating onslaught of
the enemy. Likewise, to realize that to obey God's charge
of wearing His complete armor continuously also means to
allow that armor to continuously burn off carnality.

By which have been given to us exceedingly great and
precious promises, that through these you may be
partakers of the divine nature, having escaped the
corruption that is in the world through lust. But also
for this very reason, giving all diligence, add to your
faith virtue, to virtue knowledge, to knowledge self-
control, to self-control perseverance, to perseverance
godliness, to godliness brotherly kindness, and to
brotherly kindness love. For if these things are yours
and abound, you will be neither barren nor unfruitful
in the knowledge of our Lord Jesus Christ. For he
who lacks these things is shortsighted, even to blind-
ness, and has forgotten that he was cleansed from his
old sins. Therefore, brethren, be even more diligent
to make your call and election sure, for if you do these
things you will never stumble; for so an entrance will

be supplied to you abundantly into the everlasting
kingdom of our Lord and Savior Jesus Christ.
—2 PETER 1:4–11

A further essential factor of God's glory being manifested through His consuming fire is that everything that
can be shaken in our personal kingdoms and worldly
kingdom will continue to be shaken through the fire. The
FireBride will have an ongoing and increasing need to
remember the Lord's purposes in light of His final preparations for her. In the ensuing period, only God's kingdom
will stand to remain eternally unshakeable in Him *and* in
His FireBride.

His FireBride has fully understood that it was God's love
for her that ordered the shaking. She would then be prepared by loving discipline to let go of those things that
were hindering her walk with Him by not allowing His
character to grow and be strengthened in her. She has real-
ized that the shakings were never meant to hinder her
walk, but as an all-wise, all-loving, all-knowing Bridegroom
already knew, they were *all* foreordained for her eternal
glory with Him.

The FireBride has learned to live her life honoring the
Salt Covenant between herself and her God by allowing all
the properties of the covenant to flavor everything in her
life. Of major importance to her fulfillment in Him was
learning to harness the flaming tongue by yielding again
and again to His cleansing, purifying fire, thus allowing the
voice of the Lord to divide the flames of fire in her life.

> The voice of the LORD divides the flames of fire. The
> voice of the LORD shakes the wilderness.
> —PSALM 29:7–8

By closely following the pillar of fire throughout her
journeys across the hot desert wilderness, she learned to
put down her spiritual roots ever deeper and deeper until

she was able to behold His face, His ways and His voice. She consistently and most assuredly learned:

1. To live by His greatest priority of developing and imparting His character into her life by first understanding and then incorporating His fiery divine process given for that explicit purpose.

2. To know and trust that this is His definitive plan for maturing and transforming her into the express image of His character, virtue and integrity as well as His power. To know and trust that this is the desired requisite before releasing and honoring a continuously powerful flow of the gifts of the Spirit—including the breaking of yokes, healing the sick, casting out demons and raising the dead.

3. To rejoice always in Him regardless of the severity of the trial or circumstance.

4. To pray without ceasing regardless of how impossible the enemy told her that was going to be "this time."

5. To give thanks in everything regardless of how devastating the crisis at that moment appeared.

6. To master and be at peace with those things in her heart that are God's determination and will for her life, regardless of discouragement that would seek to make itself evident in the natural.

> Rejoice always, pray without ceasing, in everything give thanks; for this is the will of God in Christ Jesus for you. Do not quench the Spirit.

Do not despise prophecies. Test all things; hold fast what is good. Abstain from every form of evil. Now may the God of peace Himself sanctify you completely; and may your whole spirit, soul, and body be preserved blameless at the coming of our Lord Jesus Christ. He who calls you is faithful, who also will do it.

—1 THESSALONIANS 5:16–24

7. To know His grace is truly never ending but constantly continues to flow and cover her, protecting as endlessly as His precious blood.

8. To find His mercies are new every morning without fail and without condemnation.

9. To learn He never expected her to follow Him flawlessly without setbacks and temporary failures, but conversely, she learned that He did consistently expect her to follow Him with complete honesty, openness and humility—without pretense or guile.

I will greatly rejoice in the LORD, my soul shall be joyful in my God; for He has clothed me with the garments of salvation, He has covered me with the robe of righteousness, as a bridegroom decks himself with ornaments, and as a bride adorns herself with her jewels.

—ISAIAH 61:10

"Lift up your eyes, look around and see; all these gather together and come to you. As I live," says the LORD, "you shall surely clothe yourself with them all as an ornament, and bind them on you as a bride does."

—ISAIAH 49:18

> He who testifies to these things says, "Surely I am coming quickly." Amen. Even so, come, Lord Jesus!
> —Revelation 22:20

What will the Lamb's wife be like? What will be the scriptural and spiritual evidence of her demeanor as she emerges from His glory fire and the wilderness that causes the Bridegroom to choose her above all others?

If we believe that the "her" in that day is synonymous by faith with the "we" in all of us, then how do we discover what the Holy Spirit has spiritually assimilated for us to learn concerning all that has been revealed and is still being revealed about her?

What are the ways of her heart that would cause her to follow not only that pillar of fire through the nighttime wilderness but to *continue* to follow Him *regardless* of what weapons the enemy formed and launched against her?

What are the characteristics that have been shaped in her so deeply and so profoundly that she would walk unceasingly until she found herself leaning totally on her Beloved, with each step in His presence, face to face, in the very midst of His glory?

Lesson From the FireBride

What has caused her heart to unquestionably and unconditionally determine and resolve that His consummate love alone is enough to keep her and fulfill her?

What are some of the secrets she has learned in her Beloved's eternal fiery presence of love that she could pass then to us who are still learning and searching for more of His Word, His Holy Spirit, His presence, His ways, His voice and His countenance?

1. She has learned that *nothing* can stop her from following Him, regardless of the cause or severity.

And they overcame him by the blood of the Lamb and by the word of their testimony, and they did not love their lives to death.

—REVELATION 12:11

Therefore we also, since we are surrounded by so great a cloud of witnesses, let us lay aside every weight, and the sin which so easily ensnares [besets] us, and let us run with endurance [patience] the race that is set before us, looking unto Jesus, the author and finisher of our faith.

—HEBREWS 12:1–2

2. She knows He will take her from strength to strength, advancing and ascending from one cherished goal to another to attain the prize of His high calling.

They go from strength to strength; each one appears before God in Zion.

—PSALM 84:7

Not that I have already attained, or am already perfected; but I press on, that I may lay hold of that for which Christ Jesus has also laid hold of me. Brethren, I do not count myself to have apprehended; but one thing I do, forgetting those things which are behind and reaching forward to those things which are ahead, I press toward the goal [mark] for the prize of the upward [high] call of God in Christ Jesus.

—PHILIPPIANS 3:12–14

3. She has learned to earnestly and deeply seek His face in the Word and prayer, receiving instruction, correction, knowledge and strategy on how

the spiritual ground can be gained and won.

> When You said, "Seek My face," my heart said to
> You, "Your face, LORD, I will seek."
> —PSALM 27:8

> Call to Me, and I will answer you, and show you
> great and mighty things, which you do not know.
> —JEREMIAH 33:3

> You will seek the LORD your God, and you will
> find Him if you seek Him with all your heart and
> with all your soul.
> —DEUTERONOMY 4:29

4. She has learned to repent immediately, thereby reclaiming any and all lost ground quickly, leaving condemnation washed by the blood and forgotten just as immediately.

> If we confess our sins, He is faithful and just to
> forgive us our sins and to cleanse us from all
> unrighteousness.
> —1 JOHN 1:9

> Do you not know that those who run in a race all
> run, but one receives the prize? Run in such a
> way that you may obtain it.
> —1 CORINTHIANS 9:24

> If we endure [suffer], we shall also reign with
> Him.
> —2 TIMOTHY 2:12

5. She has learned not only to repent quickly and put her sins and iniquities under His atoning

blood, grace and mercy, but of equal importance, to seek His wisdom to remedy future foolishness, oversights, errors and mistakes.

> Though your sins are like scarlet, they shall be white as snow; though they are red like crimson, they shall be as wool.
>
> —ISAIAH 1:18

> In Him we have redemption through His blood, the forgiveness of sins, according to the riches of His grace.
>
> —EPHESIANS 1:7

6. She has learned not just to forgive, but to move in a *spirit of forgiveness* to all others from her heart.

> Therefore if you bring your gift to the altar, and there remember that your brother has something against you, leave your gift there before the altar, and go your way. First be reconciled to your brother, and then come and offer your gift.
>
> —MATTHEW 5:23–24

> For if you forgive men their trespasses, your heavenly Father will also forgive you.
>
> —MATTHEW 6:14

> Then he knelt down and cried out with a loud voice, "Lord, do not charge them with this sin."
>
> —ACTS 7:60

7. She has learned to bless and then bless again everyone whose life she touches, especially those who despitefully use her, persecute her and revile her.

This is the way you shall bless the children of Israel. Say to them: "The LORD bless you and keep you; the LORD make His face shine upon you, and be gracious to you; the LORD lift up His countenance upon you, and give you peace."

—NUMBERS 6:23–26

But I say to you who hear: Love your enemies, do good to those who hate you, bless those who curse you, and pray for those who spitefully use you.

—LUKE 6:27–28

Bless those who persecute you; bless and do not curse.

—ROMANS 12:14

Therefore, "if your enemy is hungry, feed him; if he is thirsty, give him a drink. . . . " Do not be overcome by evil, but overcome evil with good.

—ROMANS 12:20–21

8. She has learned not to decry, doubt, dispute nor remember that which the blood had irretrievably removed from her life, as well as others' lives—specifically and particularly those things done to and against her by her trespassers.

For I will be merciful to their unrighteousness, and their sins and their lawless deeds I will remember no more.

—HEBREWS 8:12

As far as the east is from the west, so far has He removed our transgressions from us.

—PSALM 103:12

9. She has learned never to call unclean, defiled or

unfit that which He has purged, refined and cleansed.

> And a voice spoke to him again the second time, "What God has cleansed you must not call common [unclean]."
> —ACTS 10:15

> For He says to Moses, "I will have mercy on whomever I will have mercy, and I will have compassion on whomever I will have compassion."
> —ROMANS 9:15

10. She has learned to continually give mercy, His mercy having shown her it is better than sacrifice.

> For I desire mercy and not sacrifice, and the knowledge of God more than burnt offerings.
> —HOSEA 6:6

> But go and learn what this means: "I desire mercy and not sacrifice." For I did not come to call the righteous, but sinners, to repentance.
> —MATTHEW 9:13

> But if you had known what this means, "I desire mercy and not sacrifice," you would not have condemned the guiltless.
> —MATTHEW 12:7

11. She has learned to manifest her love for Him by *uncompromisingly* obeying Him.

> If you love Me, keep My commandments.
> —JOHN 14:15

> Casting down arguments and every high thing
> that exalts itself against the knowledge of God,
> bringing every thought into captivity to the obe-
> dience of Christ.
> —2 Corinthians 10:5

> And to love Him with all the heart, with all the
> understanding, with all the soul, and with all
> the strength, and to love one's neighbor as one-
> self, is more than all the whole burnt offerings
> and sacrifices.
> —Mark 12:33

12. She has learned to give without expectation of
    recognition, praise or reward from man. Her
    expectations of any or all rewards exist with her
    Lord and Bridegroom alone.

> Say to the daughter of Zion, "Surely your salva-
> tion is coming; behold, His reward is with Him,
> and His work before Him."
> —Isaiah 62:11

> No flesh should glory in His presence.
> —1 Corinthians 1:29

> I am the Lord, that is My name; and My glory I
> will not give to another, nor My praise to carved
> images.
> —Isaiah 42:8

13. She has learned to do whatever He asks uncon-
    ditionally, showing that all He will require of
    her in the final analysis is to do justly, to love
    mercy and to walk humbly with Him.

> He has shown you, O man, what is good; and

what does the LORD require of you but to do justly, to love mercy, and to walk humbly with your God?

—MICAH 6:8

14. She has learned how to lovingly give His comfort and compassion to others by reason of the fact that she had first learned how to receive them from Him—both directly and through others.

Who comforts us in all our tribulation, that we may be able to comfort those who are in any trouble, with the comfort with which we ourselves are comforted by God.

—2 CORINTHIANS 1:4

Therefore if there is any consolation in Christ, if any comfort of love, if any fellowship of the Spirit, if any affection and mercy, fulfill my joy by being like-minded, having the same love, being of one accord, of one mind.

—PHILIPPIANS 2:1–2

15. She has learned to live by His words given to her on a hillside: It is a greater and more lasting blessing to give than it is to receive.

I have shown you in every way, by laboring like this, that you must support the weak. And remember the words of the Lord Jesus, that He said, "It is more blessed to give than to receive."

—ACTS 20:35

Blessed are the poor in spirit,
    For theirs is the kingdom of heaven.
Blessed are those who mourn,
    For they shall be comforted.

Blessed are the meek,
> For they shall inherit the earth.

Blessed are those who hunger and thirst for
righteousness,
> For they shall be filled.

Blessed are the merciful,
> For they shall obtain mercy.

Blessed are the pure in heart,
> For they shall see God.

Blessed are the peacemakers,
> For they shall be called the sons of God.

Blessed are those who are persecuted for
righteousness' sake,
> For theirs is the kingdom of heaven.
>> —MATTHEW 5:3–10

There is no way we can miss what the FireBride and her Bridegroom are saying to those of us who consider ourselves to be an elect and soon-to-be-chosen member of that glorious wedding party invited to sit down at the wedding supper of the Lamb.

The one thing that remains unmistakable is His spiritual signet to all those destined for heaven: It is the Lord's character and His fruit of the Spirit. Together with His virtue and standard of loving excellence, which will eternally flow through each one, they are to be an indivisible part of the most unique, original and one-of-a-kind innumerable company that embodies His FireBride.

There will no longer be a need for the nine manifested gifts of the Holy Spirit. They were only given by the Lord to His body while here on earth as confirming evidence of His authority and power for His church. They were given as supernatural evidence to the world to confirm that the kingdom of God had come nigh them to reconcile, restore and redeem mankind.

These manifestation gifts were given for a specifically declared purpose and reason and for a specifically declared season and time. But after the last member of His FireBride has been received, there will no longer be a need for any of these gifts.

> Love never fails. But whether there are prophecies, they will fail; whether there are tongues, they will cease; whether there is knowledge, it will vanish away. For we know in part and we prophesy in part. But when that which is perfect has come, then that which is in part will be done away.
> —1 CORINTHIANS 13:8–10

The reason why these gifts will no longer be needed is at once both apparent and simple. Each member of the bride of Christ will have instantly received their total and final inheritance from the Lord as a son of God (Eph. 1:14). Each will have been inclusively and eternally transformed as a commensurate and equal partaker of God's glory and as a joint heir with Him. Therefore, each member of the bride will also be living concurrently as a son of God, joint heirs with the Lord and His ultimate energy source of eternal glorious power.

> When He is revealed, we shall be like Him.
> —1 JOHN 3:2

He has given us, as male and female members of His body, a physical natural order for protection, covering and blessing (husband and wife, those who have rule or authority, for example). This physical order has been given us—male and female alike—to teach, test and examine our obedience, which creates a bridge of His making and design by the Holy Spirit to God's transcendent spiritual order and realm where there is neither male nor female in Christ Jesus (Gal. 3:28).

Every son of God—both male and female—will have

learned to take upon himself the character of the Bridegroom through the fruit of the Spirit in order to become loving, submissive and obedient, thereby growing and maturing into the FireBride of Christ.

In the Spirit realm every member of His bride prepares herself by operating as a son of God, while every son of God prepares himself to become the FireBride of Christ by becoming submissive and lovingly obedient.

This is the last and eternal one of God's ultimate paradoxes. It is also the one of greatest importance for us to learn if we are to fully understand our rightfully appointed place in His spiritual kingdom.

He has created every female to be empowered by the Holy Spirit as a son of God while simultaneously having created every male to be the submissive and loving bride of Christ. Then both male and female are rightfully maturing not only as powerful sons of God, but also as the loving submissive FireBride of Christ.

> For as many as are led by the Spirit of God, these are sons of God.
> —ROMANS 8:14

> For you are all sons of God through faith in Christ Jesus.
> —GALATIANS 3:26

> Nor can they die anymore, for they are equal to the angels and are sons of God.
> —LUKE 20:36

> And the glory which You gave Me I have given them, that they may be one just as We are one.
> —JOHN 17:22

Christ's FireBride has learned to move with freedom in

His love and with complete liberty, under His authority while similarly honoring His commission of love, by submitting to one another, to headship and to authority (John 8:36).

> There is neither Jew nor Greek, there is neither slave nor free, there is neither male nor female; for you are all one in Christ Jesus.
> —GALATIANS 3:28

> Now the Lord is the Spirit; and where the Spirit of the Lord is, there is liberty.
> —2 CORINTHIANS 3:17

In so doing she has learned to preserve undiminished freedom in God by obeying His love charge to submit to one another and His order in the kingdom of God.

> Be kindly affectionate to one another with brotherly love, in honor giving preference to one another.
> —ROMANS 12:10

> Giving thanks always for all things to God the Father in the name of our Lord Jesus Christ, submitting to one another in the fear of God.
> —EPHESIANS 5:20–21

She has learned how to open up every aspect of her life to His incorruptible character, thereby removing every obstruction and hindrance that would prevent the pure flow of God's miraculous power in her own life and every life she touched.

> When the Lord has washed away the filth of the daughters of Zion, and purged the blood of Jerusalem from her midst, by the spirit of judgment and by the spirit of burning, then the LORD will create above

every dwelling place of Mount Zion, and above her assemblies . . . the shining of a flaming fire by night. For over all the glory there will be a covering. And there will be a tabernacle for shade in the daytime from the heat, for a place of refuge, and for a shelter from storm and rain.

—ISAIAH 4:4–6

You have come to Mount Zion and to the city of the living God, the heavenly Jerusalem, to an innumerable company of angels, to the general assembly and church of the firstborn who are registered in heaven, to God the Judge of all, to the spirits of just men made perfect.

—HEBREWS 12:22–23

And behold, I am coming quickly, and My reward is with Me, to give to every one according to his work. . . . Amen. Even so, come, Lord Jesus!

—REVELATION 22:12, 20

Bibliography

Alexander, David S. and Alexander, Pat, eds. *Eerdman's Handbook to the Bible*. Grand Rapids, MI: Wm. B. Eerdmans Publishing Co., 1983.

Barker, William P. *Everyone in the Bible*. Old Tappan, NJ: Revell, 1966.

Conner, Kevin. *Interpreting the Symbols and Types*. Portland, OR: Bible Temple Publishing, 1992.

Davis, John J. and Whitcomb, John C. *A History of Israel From Conquest to Exile*. Grand Rapids, MI: Baker Book House, 1971.

Gee, Donald. *The Fruit of the Spirit*. Springfield, MO: Gospel Publishing House, 1979.

Henry, Matthew. *Matthew Henry's Commentary on the Whole Bible*. Grandville, MI: World Bible Publishers, Inc., 1985.

Meredith, J. L. *Meredith's Book of Bible Lists*. Minneapolis, MN: Bethany House Publishers, 1980.

PC Study Bible for Windows. Seattle, WA: Biblesoft, 1992, 1995.

Richards, L. O. *Zondervan Expository Dictionary of Bible Words*. Grand Rapids, MI: Zondervan, 1985.

Roget, P. M. *International Thesaurus*. New York: Harper & Row, 1977.

Slemming, Charles W. *Thus Shall Thou Serve*. Fort Washington, PA: Christian Literature Crusade, 1992.

Sumrall, Lester. *The Gifts and Ministries of the Holy Spirit*. Springdale, PA: Whitaker House, 1993.

Wilson, Walter L. *Wilson's Dictionary of Bible Types*. Grand Rapids, MI: Wm. B. Eerdmans Publishing Co., 1957.

If you enjoyed *FireBride*, we would like to
recommend the following books:

The Heavens Opened
by Anna Rountree

Passion for Jesus
by Mike Bickle

The Power of Covenant Prayer
by Francis Frangipane

The Next Move of God
by Fuchsia Pickett

The Singing God
by Sam Storms

You can experience more of God's grace & love!

If you would like free information on how you can know God more deeply and experience His grace, love and power more fully in your life, simply write or e-mail us. We'll be delighted to send you information that will be a blessing to you.

To check out other titles from **Creation House** that will impact your life, be sure to visit your local Christian bookstore, or call this toll-free number to learn the location of the Christian retailer nearest you: **1-800-991-7747**

For free information from Creation House:

CREATION HOUSE
600 Rinehart Rd.
Lake Mary, FL 32746
www.creationhouse.com